25 YEARS

at COTON MANOR

Ian and Susie Pasley-Tyler

Susie Pasley-Tyler

Ian Pasley-Tyler

A History of Coton Manor and its Garden

Ann Beeson

A History of Coton Manor and its Garden

Ann Benson

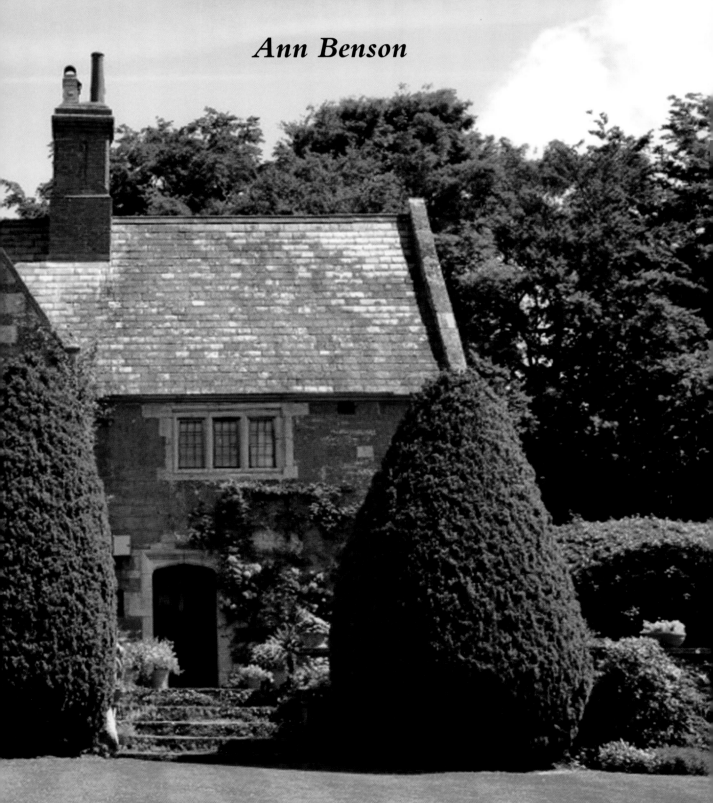

First published in 2015

© Ann Benson

ISBN 978-1-910693-17-9 (Pb)
ISBN 978-1-910693-16-2 (Hb)

British Library Cataloguing-in-Publication Data
A catalogue record for this book is available from the British Library

Typeset in Bembo

Typeset and layout by Addison Print Ltd, Northampton
Printed by Berforts Information Press Ltd, Stevenage

Dedication

For all those who love visiting Coton's Garden.
I hope this book enriches your visit.

Contents

Foreword by Ian Pasley-Tyler
ix

Preface
xi

Introduction
1

Domesday, Civil War and Restoration
7

Elizabeth and Harold Bryant
31

Haroldine and the Commander
51

Susie and Ian Pasley-Tyler
77

Susie Pasley-Tyler: a personal reflection
'Gardening to make you smile'
117

Afterword
137

Coton Plant List *139*

Author's Acknowledgements *146*

Picture Credits *147*

Coton Manor's current owner,
Ian Pasley-Tyler, as a young,
eager gardener.

Foreword

I was born at Coton many more years ago than I care to admit to. Long before the garden was opened to visitors, I enjoyed a blissful childhood here, together with my brother and sister, when it was really a huge playground for us. My boyhood at Coton was largely dominated by sports, mainly tennis. However, my regular visits to the court were often interrupted by my mother ambushing me to move a large shrub. This became a bit of a 'cat and mouse' game as being diverted to garden chores wasn't really on my agenda! In retrospect I greatly regret my indolence, as my poor mother was cultivating a very large garden more or less on her own. Our two young gardeners were persistently hijacked by my father who was always engaged on landscape projects or developing the water network in the garden. During this time I was able to observe the steady transformation of the family garden. It was a gradual evolution without the involvement of landscape designers or a grand master plan aimed at becoming a show garden. Changes to the garden have always been implemented in accordance with the family's wishes. The very personal aspect of the garden, which is often commented on by visitors, derives from this philosophy.

As shown opposite, I was introduced to gardening at an early age. However, it was not sustained. Ironically, I play only a minimal part in the gardening these days. My wife, Susie, has taken on the mantle with such zeal that I have been quietly dropped from the gardening team. I now content myself with watering duties and maintaining the Bluebell Wood. My role is largely administrative, manning the gate, selling plants and ensuring the catering operation runs smoothly. I cannot conclude this foreword without mentioning one respect in which I have enjoyed the greatest good fortune. This is Susie's absolute devotion and commitment to the garden where she strives to attain the highest possible standards throughout the year, and irrespective of the vilest of weather. Visitors often congratulate me for being clever in my choice of wife given her very obvious gardening talent. I have to counter such comments by telling them these skills were not at all apparent at the outset and never entered the equation when we decided to wed. We lived the first twenty five years of married life without any special interest in gardening but moving to Coton galvanised her latent horticultural skills and the rest, as the saying goes, is history.

Ian Pasley-Tyler
Coton Manor, May 2015.

The author's mother, Sophia Haywood (1916–2011),
enjoying a visit to Coton's Bluebell Wood in 2008.
Sophia was a great gardener and loved history.

Preface

A garden that lifts the spirit often defies explanation. I still remember my first visit to Coton Manor Garden in the early 1990s and being immediately affected by its therapeutic atmosphere. It spoke to me on several levels. Yes, it was immaculately maintained and showcased an impressive collection of plants flowing effortlessly across ten acres. But the whole effect was, and still is, greater than its horticultural parts. Coton's intangible quality has drawn me to return again and again, and the same can be said of the thousands who annually visit this corner of the rolling Northamptonshire countryside.

My mother and I came regularly to Coton to enjoy its garden and the delights of its Café. Alzheimers prevented 'normal' conversation in the last years of her life but the shared experiences of being surrounded by pink roses, her favourite, and a sea of blue flowers in the Manor's Bluebell Wood, enabled us to connect with each other in a way that did not require words. Since she died I have returned many times, at first, if I'm honest, as a means of rekindling memories of her. More recently, and after becoming a designed landscape historian, I've begun to see Coton anew and wonder how it came to develop into the sublime space that now resonates with its many visitors.

So I started to use my skills as an academic to reveal the history of Coton Manor. When I approached Coton's owners to establish the extent to which they would give me access to their family records, if indeed these existed, I was greeted with open arms. They had wanted to write the history themselves but sufficient time to do so never seemed to be available. At times my sleuthing has been frustrating with too many blind alleys to mention, but overall, it has been an enormously enjoyable experience. It has taken me to an inordinate number and variety of locations, including the British Library, the National Archives, local Record Offices and stately homes such as Holdenby House some five miles from Coton. Throughout it all, Coton's owners have provided me with accommodation in their lovely home, fed me and generally been as supportive as I could ever have hoped for. The people who work at Coton have generously given of their time and memories. Friends have provided thoughtful and informed encouragement; in particular, Marilyn Lister, Michele Bradley and Dr Charles Moseley, have supported my endeavours with skill and affectionate enthusiasm.

I've written this book in order to share with others what I've found out about Coton Manor in the hope that it will further enhance peoples' enjoyment of the garden. I like to think that my mother would have loved reading it too.

Dr Ann Benson
Monmouthshire, 2015.

Introduction

At 11a.m. on Saturday, 22 February the wooden gates at Coton Manor, near Guilsborough, Northamptonshire, open to admit the first garden visitors of 2014. After the wettest January on record and the worst flooding across the UK within living memory, the weather has mellowed at last to provide a sunny welcome at Coton. Snowdrops and hellebores are in full flower and the garden is looking as immaculate as ever. Owners Ian and Susie Pasley-Tyler brace themselves for what promises to be a busy day as the improved weather is likely to draw people out of their homes. Visitors will be eager to see the signs of early spring in Coton's garden.

Ian is on duty at the entrance and today he is very ably assisted by grandson, Harry, who at age 10 years seems to have inherited the Pasley-Tyler business acumen and charm. He adds up admission prices and works out the change like a machine. His accompanying puppy is

Ian Pasley-Tyler and grandson, Harry, welcome the first visitors of 2014 to Coton.

stroked by a visitor who says, "that's very therapeutic" to which Harry immediately replies, "I hope you find the garden therapeutic too." Meanwhile, Susie, ever the hands-on gardener, is absorbed in weeding around a clump of the shrub rose, *Rosa chinensis* 'Mutabilis', which will have its delicate, single flowers gloriously varying from yellow to shades of pink in summer.

Mike and Jenny Joannou are first through the gates today. They have been visiting Coton Manor for over thirty years. Initially, they came to search for a particular plant in Coton's nursery, during which their young children were entertained by the wildfowl roaming Goose Park. "A friend of ours was a keen gardener and was impressed by a particular type of *Rodgersia* called *pinnatum* 'Superba', which we thought would be a suitable birthday present for her. We searched everywhere for a supplier of this plant and then discovered it was available at Coton. Our friend was delighted with it. We've been coming to Coton ever since, it's so beautiful and peaceful here, they grow lots of unusual plants in their Nursery, and we love the Café. There's always something of interest in the garden, whatever the season."

The Wayman family:
three generations of Coton visitors.

Ruth Wayman has also been visiting Coton for more than thirty years. Today she is accompanied by her son and daughter-in-law, and three month old grand-daughter, Florence. The grass paths are overlaid with mats to prevent people sliding and slipping after the weeks of heavy rain, and Florence's pram glides easily around the garden. Ruth says, "I love the

Sunshine and Snowdrops.

quietness of this garden. It's not overly commercial and it feels like someone's home – which it is. The Bluebell Wood is my favourite, and I like to buy plants here because they always grow well in my garden." No doubt in the years to come Florence will visit Coton and remember that her grandmother thought it a special place.

Everyone is cheered by the improved weather and the opportunity to get out and about. The snowdrops and hellebores steal the show and many pots of these are sold by the Nursery. When visitors are asked what it is about Coton that tempts them back again and again they refer to its beauty, peacefulness, and a host of other features but they usually finish with phrases such as 'it just makes us feel good' and 'we feel relaxed here'. As regular visitors, Ida and Geoffrey Snushall say, "Coton isn't a show garden despite it being immaculately maintained and being open to the public for most of the year. It still feels like someone's home; it doesn't overwhelm. All the different areas just blend together – it's impressive but somehow comfortable at the same time."

How does one explain Coton's attraction? Certainly the honey-coloured seventeenth-century manor house provides an attractive background for the climbing purple wisteria, pink roses and evergreens. The house also introduces an element of romanticism. One could be scientific about it all and use Christopher Alexander's reasons for why certain things impart a sense of well-being.[1] However, referring to an achieved balance of formal and informal spaces, proportions, mass and void, light and darkness, and rhythms in planting schemes still doesn't seem an adequate explanation of Coton's charm. Although there is some formality in the garden, particularly in the old Rose Garden near the Loggia, overall, the garden celebrates its location. It embraces rather than fights the natural changes in ground levels, springs and distant views. Perhaps Alexander Pope in Epistle IV of his Moral Essays explains Coton's success in using the natural landscape in its garden design:

In all, let Nature never be forgot,
But treat the goddess like a modest fair,
Nor over-dress, nor leave wholly bare; let not each beauty everywhere be spied,
Where half the skill is decently to hide.
He gains all points who pleasingly confounds,
Surprises, varies and conceals the bounds.
Consult the genius of the place in all …[2]

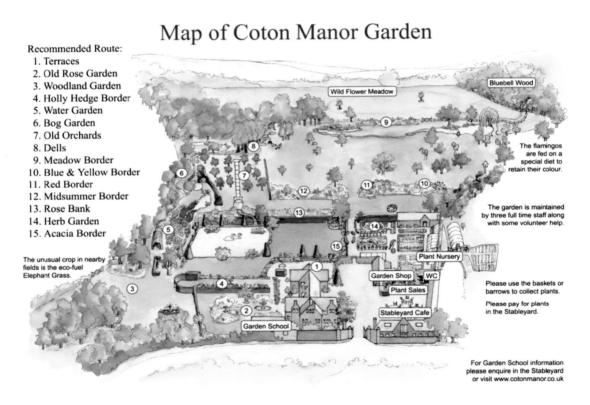

Map of Coton Manor Garden

Recommended Route:
1. Terraces
2. Old Rose Garden
3. Woodland Garden
4. Holly Hedge Border
5. Water Garden
6. Bog Garden
7. Old Orchards
8. Dells
9. Meadow Border
10. Blue & Yellow Border
11. Red Border
12. Midsummer Border
13. Rose Bank
14. Herb Garden
15. Acacia Border

Bluebell Wood

Wild Flower Meadow

The flamingos are fed on a special diet to retain their colour.

The garden is maintained by three full time staff along with some volunteer help.

The unusual crop in nearby fields is the eco-fuel Elephant Grass.

Plant Nursery

Garden Shop   WC

Plant Sales

Please use the baskets or barrows to collect plants.

Please pay for plants in the Stableyard.

Stableyard Cafe

Garden School

For Garden School information please enquire in the Stableyard or visit www.cotonmanor.co.uk

Complimentary Map, 2014 – will this become an old estate map in future years?

Ian and Susie are the third generation within Ian's family to live at Coton. Clearly, they love their home and this is reflected in their personal involvement in the garden's maintenance and public opening. Do visitors absorb that love and is this at least partly responsible for Coton's appeal? On this cold day in February Coton's owners take it in turns to warm themselves and fortify with food but, as always, at least one member of the family is on duty at the entrance to greet and bid farewell to visitors. Are they alone responsible for creating Coton's garden that lifts and comforts the heart in equal measures? Has the garden changed across time? Who built the house which intriguingly has the initials, W, E and H carved into its stone alongside the date, 1662? Are these the marks of Coton's architect or its owners at this time and did a house exist before the Civil War?

This book provides answers to these questions – and others. In so doing, the history of Coton Manor and its garden is revealed through the people whose lives have been woven into their fabric. So, what is Coton's history?

NOTES

1   Alexander, Christopher, *The Nature of Order: The Phenomenon of Life* (Berkley, California: The Centre for Environmental Structure, 2002). In chapter five of this book Alexander adopts a scientific view of the world to explore the properties of life and what gives beauty, life and functionality to our surroundings.

2   From *An Epistle to Lord Burlington 'Of the Use of Riches'*. 1731.

The alcove by Coton Manor's 1662 door.

Domesday, Civil War and Restoration

The hamlet of Coton lies less than half a mile south of Guilsborough. At an unknown date Coton was transferred from the parish of Guilsborough to that of Ravensthorpe where it has remained to this day. This transfer accounts for the very irregular shape of the Ravensthorpe parish where Coton's lands extend towards the north-east as a narrow wedge (see medieval settlements and estates overleaf). Some evidence suggests the transfer dates to a time when plague was rife in Coton, and Guilsborough did not wish to accommodate the dead in its burial areas. This is unlikely, not least because if the population had been in the middle of the plague crisis, there simply would have been neither time nor inclination to go through the convoluted legal process of parish transfer. A more likely reason is that the transfer of Coton with its tithes from Guilsborough to Ravensthorpe was the result of the need to provide income for an incumbent / the church of Ravensthorpe. What is certain is that in the most ancient documents the settlement of Coton is aligned with the parish of Guilsborough and not with that of Ravensthorpe.

Coton's history dates back at least to the eleventh century and is initially peppered with feudal terms. The Domesday survey of 1086 records a manor of Coton being owned by William Peverel (c.1040–c.1115), also known as William Peverell the Elder, a Norman knight listed in the Roll of Battle Abbey as a companion of William the Conqueror at Hastings in 1066. Peveril Castle, standing high above the pretty village of Castleton in the heart of Derbyshire's Peak District, is most likely the main home of the Peverels during this period. However, at the time of the Conqueror's survey, William Peverel received 15 shillings for the entire manor of Coton (variously called Cota, Cote, Cotes and Cotton across the centuries). The manor consisted of three virgates and a half. Although varying in size from area to area even within the same manor, a virgate was approximately 30 acres. By the time the Domesday was completed, William was receiving 30 shillings, which included four shillings yearly rent from Coton's water-driven corn mill.

At this time the arable land associated with the manor amounted to three carucates, where a carucate was a measurement of land equal to the amount of terrain that a team of eight oxen could reasonably work over the course of a year. Like other medieval land measurements, the

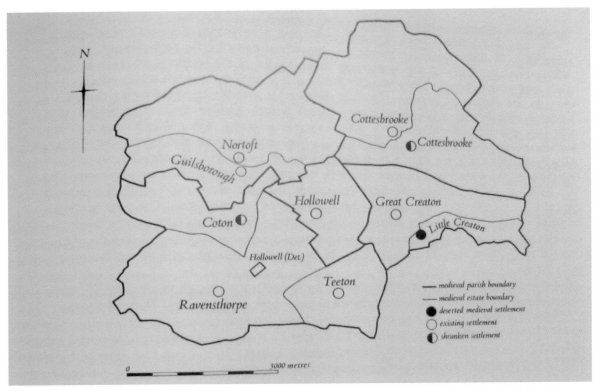

Medieval settlements and estates: Cottesbrooke, Creaton, Guilsborough, Hollowell
and Ravensthorpe.
George Baker, *History and Antiquities of the County of Northampton*,
(London: Bower Nicols & Son and Rodwell, 1822-1830), p.xiv.

carucate could vary depending on the type of land involved but generally approximated to
100 acres. Two of the three carucates were in demesne, a word from the Old French *demeine*
(later Anglo-Norman French *demesne*) meaning 'belonging to a lord'. This simply means that
this part of the arable land was attached to the manor house and retained by the then owner,
William Peverel, for his own use as he wished. Because labour was cheap, there were ample
advantages in cultivating the demesne. In addition, it's recorded at this time that three servants,
one maiden, one villein (a farm servant who was legally tied to a lord of the manor) and four
cottagers had half a carucate within the manor.

In 1220 the manor of Coton was known as Cota de Goldington, being then in the
possession of Peter de Goldington. In 1250, when Henry III had been on the English throne
for 35 years, Peter de Goldington obtained a grant of free warren for the manor of Cota. Free
warren, often just written as *warren*, refers to a type of franchise or privilege conveyed by a
sovereign to a person in mediaeval England. It promises to hold the person harmless for killing
game of certain species (hare, rabbit, pheasant, partridge) within a stipulated area, usually a
wood. The receiver of this privilege was granted an exemption from the law under which all
game in the realm were the property of the sovereign. However, the privilege of free warren
was a reciprocal relationship. The receiver of the privilege had to take on the role of steward

on behalf of the sovereign and ensure the protection of the game from all others who might wish to hunt it. So, within the lands associated with the manor of Cota (Coton) at this time, there was a wood in which the owner hunted rabbits for food and fur. It is tempting to speculate on the wood existing near today's Coton Manor house as being the same wood – but more on this wood later.

In about 1259, and still within the reign of Henry III, Simon de Thorp is recorded as dying whilst owning land in Cotes and Ravensthorpe which he held *in capite* by a knight's fee. A knight's fee was a unit measure of land deemed sufficient to support a knight. Of necessity, it would not only provide sustenance for himself and his attendants but also the means to furnish himself and his equipage with horses and armour to fight for his overlord in battle. No cash rent was payable. Therefore, Simon de Thorp possessed land within Cotes (Coton) in exchange for supplying the King with a number of armed horsemen as and when required.

Due to a dispute which is recorded in 1259, it appears that this land in Simon de Thorp's possession was not the whole of the manor of Cotes. A family quarrel between Alan Fitz-Roald and his wife, Maud, and Alan's daughter, Isabella, about the ownership of a dwelling house, land, a wood and the mill within Cotes – a description of what would have been the manor of Cotes - resulted in fines being levied against Alan. He had attempted to prevent Isabella from possessing the estate. However, with Isabella dying without children and he surviving her, by about 1279 in the reign of Edward I (Edward Longshanks), Alan is recorded as possessing the property of Cotes by one knight's fee.

Richard Champernon is the next person associated with possessing the manor of Cotes towards the end of the reign of Edward III (d.1377). In 1379, the second year of Richard II's reign, the manor was seized into the hands of the Crown due to Richard Champernon selling it without the necessary licence from the King. Some sixty years later, in about 1444, when Henry IV was King, the manor of Cotes was restored to Roger Champernon as the rightful heir, and then by succession to John Champernon. John died in the 1470s in the reign of Edward IV and left his estate to his two daughters, Blanche the wife of Sir Robert Wyloughby, and Joan Champernon, a minor aged eleven years. The manor of Cotes appears to have first passed to Joan, the younger daughter, who later married a man called Talbott. When Joan died in about 1506 towards the end of the reign of Henry VII, the estate passed to her next heir, Robert Willougby Lord Broke, the son of Blanche, her sister.

A Richard Samwell is then recorded as holding 120 acres of arable land, 20 acres of meadow, one water-mill and two messuages, where a messuage was usually a dwelling house together with its outbuildings and adjacent land. In effect, this holding was the manor of Cotes. Richard held this by fealty of Lord Broke, Blanche's son. Fealty was a key feature of feudalism in medieval England, and Europe as a whole. The swearing of fealty took the form of an oath by a subordinate to his Lord. Richard Samwell would have sworn to remain faithful to Lord Broke and to fulfil certain duties under this Lord's protection, which here consisted of Richard holding the manor of Cotes and farming its lands without payment. Richard died in about 1520 and left the manor to his son, Francis Samwell, then aged five years, when Henry VIII was King.

Now the history of the manor of Coton becomes unclear, with seemingly contradictory accounts. According to the records of the College of Arms, there have been people called Dickins at Ravensthorpe near Coton since 1354. A Henry Dycon of Ravensthorpe was born about 1470 when Edward IV was King. At an unknown date he 'purchased from the William de Broke family the lease of Coton Manor House with all of its manorial rights and lands in Ravensthorpe, Thurnby, Tekon, Assheby, Holwell, Nortaft and Wynnewyk', all within a six-mile radius. This purchase is stated in an unpublished pamphlet about the history of the Dickins family. The claim at least seems plausible because of its reference to the de Broke family as known owners of the manor of Coton during the end of the fifteenth and the beginning of the sixteenth centuries. However, the pamphlet also states that this property, after passing to Henry's widow, Alice, and his son, John, remained in the family for nearly 200 years which is at odds with other records of Coton's ownership described below. The pamphlet records 1630 as the latest date by which the family are parties to a grant of Coton manor, and after 1717 they no longer write themselves as 'of Coton'. The 1937 east window inserted in the early fourteenth-century church of St. Denys in Ravensthorpe commemorates members of the Dickins family and shows the Dickins' Crest and Coat of Arms. Certainly people named Dickins, variously also known as Dickens, Dykins, Dykyns and Dycons, have lived in Ravensthorpe, Coton and nearby villages for many centuries; a Sir William Dykyns is also listed as a chaplain in Ravensthorpe in 1534 and was buried in the churchyard there in 1556. William carries the title, Sir, as a courtesy for being a priest. Before the dissolution of the monasteries by Henry VIII, the knights hospitallers of Jerusalem had the patronage of Ravensthorpe church and are also recorded as owning some land in Coton. After the suppression of the monasteries this patronage passed to the Dean and Canons of Christ Church, Oxford.

The Dickins' connection with the manor of Coton from the mid-sixteenth century seems at odds with other records. By the reign of Edward VI and so between 1547 and 1553, there was a dispute between Hugh Foxton and Sir Fulk Grevill over the possession of the 'manor of Cotton under Guilsborough'. In the same year there was another argument about the manor's possession between Sir Fulk Grevill and a Thomas Andrews. On both occasions fines were levied and Sir Fulk Grevill appears to have lost control of Cotton. He was Philip Syney's biographer and school friend. In 1564, when Elizabeth was Queen, it is claimed that Dame Katherine Andrewes died in possession of the manor and that it then passed to Thomas Andrewes, her son and heir, who was later knighted. An inquest then certified that the manor was held of the Crown *in capite* by knight's service. According to the feudal system, all lands in England were considered as held of the king, who is styled lord paramount. A tenant on land held of the

The Dickens' Crest.
By kind permission of Dennis Patrick.

Crown, however, was considered as having permanent possession of the land. Sir Fulk Grevill appears to have finally secured possession of the manor of Coton by the beginning of the seventeenth century and it then descended to his successors and heirs which included the Verney family. Richard Verney (1621-1711) was summoned to parliament by the title, Lord Willoughby de Broke, in 1693 and was the owner of the manor of Coton at this time. The Verney Papers capture the history of the Verneys and other families connected with them in the seventeenth century and may be readily accessed online.

Genealogical records for the Fulk Grevill, Verney, and Willoughby the Lords Broke families clearly show they are related but no mention is made of the Dickins family in any of its various forms of spelling. So whether the Dickins family owned the manor of Coton, were tenants of it or merely owned some land in Coton, remains unclear. What is certain is that whoever owned or occupied the manor of Coton, they would have seen the property ravaged during the English Civil War (1642–1651). The New Model Army moved into Northamptonshire in the summer of 1645. They made their way through Coton on route to Naseby to engage the royalists in what would become a battle of epic proportions on the 14th of June 1645 (see overleaf).

Parliamentary soldiers were quartered in and around Guilsborough the night before the battle while Cromwell was in the vanguard based one mile further north. There would have been thousands of soldiers sleeping in the fields around Coton and accounts show that houses were commandeered and coal, wood, food, drink and animals were plundered from Coton's residents. With so many soldiers descending on a village it must have been impossible to enforce full discipline. Guilsborough villagers also recorded the loss of sheep and lambs, household goods and food, as well as hedges, turves and gates being burnt for camp fires, and straw, grass and oats taken for horses. Following the parliamentary victory, the greater part of the New Model Army marched northwards towards Leicester. Like many royalist establishments, Coton Manor was razed to the ground.

Enter Oliver Cromwell (1599-1658) as Lord Protector during the Commonwealth period (1649-1660). It is well-documented that during the Commonwealth many parliamentary soldiers had arrears of pay. Debentures allowed soldiers to use their accumulated arrears to buy Crown lands. Some soldiers obtained property which they then dismantled to sell the associated building materials and fittings – making not inconsiderable fortunes in the process. In these respects Adam Baynes was supremely able. Born in 1622 and from a family of wealthy York merchants, he entered the army of the parliament and rose to the rank of captain serving under Fairfax and Lambert. He sat in three protectorate parliaments as MP for Leeds whilst making large purchases of land for Lambert and himself. He appears to have trafficked largely in the purchase of forfeited estates, buying among others several royal forests in Lancashire, the estate of Wimbledon, and Queen Henrietta's domain of Holdenby (Holmby), some four miles from Coton. At the Restoration in 1660 he was deprived of some of his acquisitions, but his circumstances continued to be affluent. In 1666, when the authorities feared an anti-royalist rising, Baynes, who had for some time been suspected of plotting against the government, was among those arrested and imprisoned in the Tower for 'treasonable practices'. He died at his estate of Knowstropp, near Leeds, Yorkshire, in December 1670.

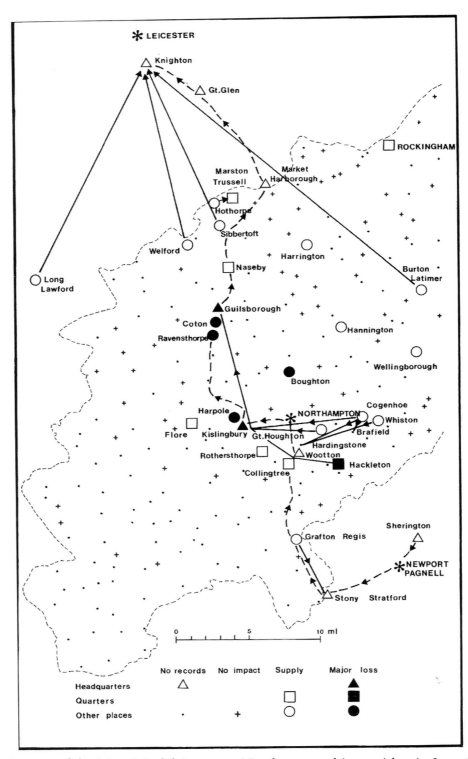

The impact of the New Model Army on Northamptonshire parishes in June 1645.
By kind permission of Glenn Foard, *Naseby*
(Barnsley: Pen & Sword Military, 2004), p.170.

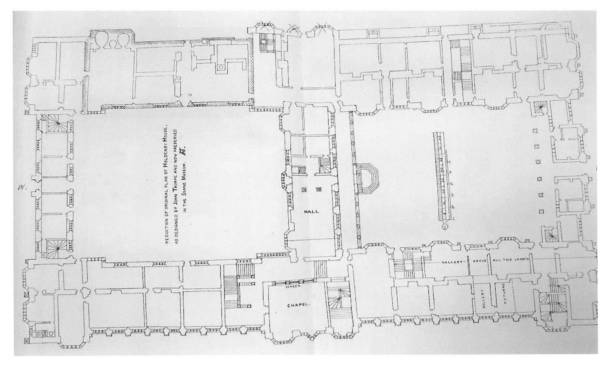

The part of Holdenby House left standing by Baynes (highlighted).
Adapted by the author from Albert Hartshorne, 'Plan of Holdenby House' in *Historical Memorials of Northampton* by Charles Hartshorne (London: Harrison and Sons, 1908), p. 12.

Holdenby was a massive palace created in about 1583 by Sir Christopher Hatton, Lord Chancellor of England during the reign of Elizabeth I. The Palace was designed for Hatton by the architect, John Thorpe, one of the most celebrated architects of his age and the builder of nearly all the grand English houses of that period. On Hatton's death the whole of the Holdenby estate passed to the Crown. In 1647 the Parliamentary Government equipped the Palace as a place of detention for Charles 1. He was detained there for several months during the summer of that year until he was taken to London by parliamentary soldiers. Following the Civil War temporary custody of the Palace was given to Thomas Lord Grey of Groby in Leicestershire, one of the most active parliamentarians. However, as the antiquarian Charles Hartshorne notes in his *Historical Memorials of Northampton*, (1848):

the trustees for the sale of Crown lands, by deed dated 5th May, 1650,
sold to [Captain] Adam Baynes of Knowsthrope, Yorkshire for £22,299. 6s. 10d,
the capital messuage or royal mansion-house of Holdenby, with its
appurtenances, gardens, orchards, and walks, containing in the whole by
estimation 38 acres 1 rood, of the present value of £26. 2s. 6d.; and the
materials of the mansion are stated in the particulars of sale to be worth £6000.
over and above the expense of taking them down.

Demolition of the Palace was a condition of the sale. All but the kitchen wing was demolished in the 1650s. This wing was approximately just one eighth of the mass of Hatton's original house and it was retained as living quarters by Baynes.

In 1660 the Holdenby estate was restored to the Crown, but for two centuries there was no resident squire, though considerable ruins remained. Of these the most architecturally important are the two archways bearing the date 1583, and a third, to the north of the house, dated 1659 and probably built by Baynes to give access to his living quarters. The Palace ruins have all been cleared except for these now free-standing arches and some garden wall foundations. In 1873-75 and 1887-88 a new house, one eighth of the size of the original palace, was built incorporating part of that left standing by Baynes. Holdenby Palace is now referred to as Holdenby House, although locals refer to it as Holmby.

It is common knowledge amongst the older inhabitants of Northamptonshire that many houses in the county lay claim to either being built from Holdenby Palace's stone or having remnants of its fittings. With the level of demolition conducted by Baynes on Hatton's massive palace, and his ability to make money from salvage activities, this is understandable. Early editions of the *Northampton Mercury* even advertised properties in Northampton as being built from Holdenby's stone, for example, Mr Markam's in St. Giles Street was advertised by the name of 'Little Holmby'. Mr Munday's in Gold Street and Miss Fawcett's in the Drapery are also often quoted in antiquarian books as being built from Holdenby's stone. In 1662 a new manor house was built at Coton to replace the house razed to the ground by parliamentary soldiers on the night before the battle at Naseby. This 1662 build is only part of the current house at Coton and is that which faces Coton's large pond; the rest of the current house was built in the early twentieth century and its story is told in the following chapter. The 1662 part of Coton Manor may well have been built from Holdenby stone.

Despite extensive searches, no sales particulars or other documentary evidence of Coton Manor being built from Holdenby stone have been traced but architecturally it is certainly possible. In an upstairs room of Coton's 1662 building there is a fireplace with a stone over-mantle that is a section of an external metope frieze that would have previously belonged to a very grand house. The quality of the carving on this stone is exceptional and in keeping with what Holdenby's famous architect, John Thorpe, would have designed. The frieze is also of similar colour to the stone that remains of the original Holdenby Palace. When the grandparents of Coton's current owners bought the Manor in 1926, this over-mantle was covered up and painted blue.

The overmantle shows a decorated ox skull (bucranium) draped with garlands. This was a Roman motif drawn from marble altars which have survived. The motif was later used on Renaissance, Baroque and Neoclassical buildings. The bucranium and the flower (rosette) are classical motifs frequently seen on historically important Tudor and Stuart buildings and can still be seen on a frieze designed specifically for the gateway at Winwick Manor House, some five miles from Coton. The decorated stone over-mantle was not designed for the fireplace at Coton. It is clearly a re-cycled section cut from a larger piece where the cut end is on the left side of the fireplace. This is also indicated by the uneven number and placing of the triglyphs

Stone over-mantle at Coton Manor.
A remnant of a metope frieze that decorated the external walls of Holdenby Palace?

(these are the small vertical columns of stone) and that nothing on the over-mantle lines up with the mid-point of the fireplace below. It is more than likely that when the person(s) who wished to build a house at Coton in 1662 saw this fine remnant of Holdenby Palace's glory days, they thought it would do very nicely over the fireplace in their new reception room. Similar bucranium features are to be seen on the 1904 outbuilding at Holdenby, placed there in commemoration of Holdenby's Tudor roots.

Commemorative bucranium decorations on Holdenby's 1904 outbuilding.
By kind permission of Holdenby's current owner,
Mr James Lowther.

Rosette on downpipes at Holdenby House.
By kind permission of Holdenby's current owner, Mr James Lowther.

The flower (rosette) motif seen on the over-mantle is to be found on the few remaining original lead downpipes of Holdenby House. More recently added pipes have reproductions of the original motif.

The same rosette motif is also found within a metope frieze on the rood screen currently located within the church at Holdenby. This screen is known to have originally been within the Palace where it was positioned between the chapel and the hall.

Screen in Holdenby's Church.

Drawing of the screen showing the metope frieze with its rosettes.
Albert Hartshorne, 'Plan of Holdenby House' in *Historical Memorials of Northampton* by Charles Hartshorne (London: Harrison and Sons, 1908), p.60.

A rosette is found on a stone placed in the middle of the 1662 gable end of Coton Manor. Its high position makes it difficult to photograph but even so, the quality of the carving is evident and indicates a high level of workmanship. It is also crafted from oölite stone rather than the less valued iron-stone. Did this come from Holdenby?

Arguably, the most persuasive evidence supporting Coton's claim for its 1662 section being built from Holdenby Palace stone is the nature of the stone itself. Pevsner refers to Coton Manor House as Coton Hall when writing in 1973. He describes the Hall as having 'gables – one banded in iron-stone and grey oölite (the shell outlines just visible to the naked eye) – and mullioned windows'.

Rosette on the 1662 gable end of Coton Manor.
INSERT The rosette on Coton's overmantle

The layering of the honey-coloured iron-stone with the almost white oölite stone, which in places clearly shows outlines of shells, is characteristic of sixteenth- and seventeenth-century houses of quality in this part of England. Layering of this type is seen in the remains of Holdenby and the estate buildings near the house. The colours and textures of these two types of stone at Holdenby and Coton are very similar. At Coton the pale grey oölite, which would have been more expensive than the iron-stone, is used sparingly and predominantly as a decorative feature.

Iron-stone and oölite. *TOP* Holdenby's estate cottages. *BOTTOM* Coton Manor.

The only evidence to suggest Coton was rebuilt in 1662 is the inscribed stone in the gable end of the house, and this seems to be contemporary with the gable wall and not inserted at a different time. The date is accompanied by the initials, WEH. These are most likely the initials of the people commissioning the build, with W being for a male, E for his wife, and the H placed above WE, their shared surname, for example William and Elizabeth Hall. This was not an uncommon practice during the seventeenth century. So who were W and EH? With no known surviving seventeenth-century documents relating to Coton Manor's purchase or building, a variety of archive material was searched for connections between the manor of Coton and these initials. Sheep tax and hearth tax records were first investigated for those who lived in the village of Coton at this time and in previous years.

Inscribed stone on Coton Manor House.

A transcription of the 1547 Northants sheep census (Brit Lib Additional Doc 25084) for the Coton area is as follows:

'A Booke of all the Townes and Hundereds with Pastures in the West Devision For the Provision

Coton und[er] Guyllesbrughe [*but no individual ratings or total are given*]
John Lucas
Rychard Lucas
Alys Dykons
Willm Hollys
... ...
Pastures Parkes and Ffedings for Cattall in the Est p[ar]te of Northampton
... ...
Coton [*but no ratings or total are given*] "

This is, in effect, a list of all the relatively wealthy people living at Coton in 1547 and interestingly there is a family with a surname beginning with H (Hollys) and a Christian name beginning with W (William). With the same Christian names passing through families from one generation to the next during at least the sixteenth and seventeenth centuries, it could well be that Coton's WH is a descendant of this William Hollys in 1547. Furthermore, families did not move around the country as they do now: it is likely that the families listed in this 1547 sheep tax record had several subsequent generations remaining in Coton or certainly in nearby villages. Of note is the inclusion of a Dykons (Alice), given the confusion of Dickins' ownership of the manor of Coton described earlier. Certainly, a relatively wealthy Dickins family lived in Coton in 1547 and most likely continued to do so for a period despite their main location then passing to Ravensthorpe village.

In the 1540s sheep were taxed on their numbers and their wool. By 1564 the sheep / wool industry was falling into decline. This largely happened because more people started to keep sheep as English wool was much prized and sold well; this led to sheep being kept in higher density in fields, and this in turn produced poorer quality wool. By the mid- to late-1600s the sheep / wool industry had collapsed. Poorer wool could not be worked on the looms as before when England was known for its high quality of this product. Broad cloth was the poorer quality woven wool cloth. This decline all happened in Elizabeth's reign and results in no sheep tax records for the period leading up to the rebuilding of a manor house in Coton in 1662.

The hearth tax was levied between 1662 and 1689 on each householder according to the number of hearths in his or her dwelling. Hearth tax records for Coton survive in part for the seventeenth century and that for 1674 lists a man called Hall as paying tax on three hearths. His Christian name is unclear in the records, possibly William or Mathew. So he could provide the correct initials for Coton's WEH 1662 stone, although this individual did not show up on the earlier sheep tax records. Perhaps he is a relatively new occupant of Coton after the Civil War. The same hearth tax record also lists a Nicholas Hollis with one hearth and a William Dickens with three hearths. The larger the number of hearths, the more substantial is the dwelling. An even earlier hearth tax record for Coton dated 1669-70 is barely readable but also appears to list these men each with the same record of hearths, although the Christian name of Hall looks more like Matthew than William. So a William Hall may be the WH on Coton's 1662 building.

Manor of Coton Suit Roll 27th October 1721 (left-hand column).
By kind permission of Northamptonshire Record Office (NPL 1439).

Whomever the initials WEH refer to on Coton's inscribed stone, and whether they were owners of this parcel of land within Coton manor or merely tenants, by 1721 the ownership of the whole manor of Coton is attributed to a widowed Lady Verney, who had been the wife of Richard Verney, Lord Willoughby de Broke. She called her court at Coton, although she resided elsewhere. The manor court was the lowest court of law in England and governed those areas over which the lord of the manor had jurisdiction; it applied only to those who resided in or held lands within the manor. The court met every three weeks throughout the year, although meetings could be more irregular than this. These courts dealt with copyhold land transfers, managing the open fields, settling disputes between individuals and manorial offences. A suit roll was kept for the homage sworn by tenants; if they were absent, a fine would be imposed. In a large manor, the steward would summon the court by instructing manorial officers to fix a notice to the church door or have it read out in church. While in theory all men over 12 attended each court, it is likely that in practice only the manorial officers, offenders, jurymen, witnesses, litigants and pledges and those involved in land transfers came to the court.

The Manorial Suit Roll of 27th October 1721 lists nine people from Coton and it is interesting to see a William Dickins and an Alice Dickins, widow, amongst these. However, there is no Hall or Hollis listed. Other Court Rolls associated with Coton survive for the period 1679-1739 (Northamptonshire Record Office, CAM 1036). These record several Hall and Hollis men, the latter variously also written as Holles and Hollys, but none called William. John and Richard frequently appear as Christian names for men in the Hollis family and during 1677 - 1687 a Richard Hollis of Coton moved to nearby Nortoft. A Michael Hollis also lived in Coton in 1692.

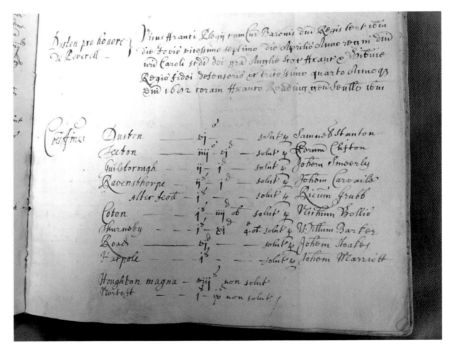

Court Roll of 1692 listing Michael Hollis of Coton.
By kind permission of Northamptonshire Record Office (CAM 1036).

The men called Hall are most often associated with the names of Richard and Vincent and a Richard Hall appears as an officer of the Court called at Coton in the late seventeenth century. Parish registers for Ravensthorpe and Guilsborough are dotted with members of the Hollis and Hall families but none with a Christian name beginning with W other than a William Hollis who appears to have had many children baptized in the late 1590s. He is unlikely to have survived until 1662 when he would have been at least well into his 80s – unlikely but just possible.

However, tantalizingly, there is some evidence for the existence of a William and Elizabeth Hollis during the early years of the Civil War. In 1643 Parliament set up two committees, the Sequestration Committee which confiscated the estates of the Royalists who fought against Parliament, and the Committee for Compounding with Delinquents which allowed Royalists whose estates had been sequestrated, to compound for their estates — pay a fine and recover their estates — if they pledged not to take up arms against Parliament again. The size of the fine they had to pay depended on the worth of the estate and how great their support for the Royalist cause had been. To administer the process of sequestration, a sequestration committee was established in each county. If a local committee sequestrated an estate they usually let it to a tenant and the income was used 'to the best advantage of the State'. If a 'delinquent' wished to recover his estate he had to apply to the Committee for Compounding with Delinquents based in London, as the national Sequestration Committee was absorbed by the Committee for Compounding in 1644. After the Restoration of the monarchy in 1660, most of the sequestrated land was returned to the pre-war owners.

The State Papers for sequestration are housed at the National Archives. They contain a reference to a Mrs Elizabeth Holles asking the Committee on 16th September 1646 for maintenance for herself and her children (SP20/2/p.497), and a separate reference to a William Holles (SP20/2/p.497). Are these people related and are they WEH who in the early years of the Restoration, built a house decorated with bands of iron-stone and oölite, ornamented with classical motifs and a date of 1662? The sleuthing continues … Whomever the initials WEH refer to on Coton's gable wall, they are more than likely to have been tenants as the ownership of the manor of Coton continued to lie with the Verneys, Lords Willoughby de Broke during the Restoration until eventually passing by marriage to the Boughton-Leighs who would hold it until the early twentieth century.

Did WEH build the 1662 house on the same footprint as that which existed before it was slighted the night before the battle of Naseby? This part of Coton Manor house does not appear to have been built on pre-existing foundations as one might expect if it were merely a replacement for what was destroyed. It is unlikely that the foundations of the pre-Civil War house would have been removed. If the 1662 manor house was built on the same site as its predecessor, it is of a different size and shape to the original. Guilsborough, Coton and Nortoft were inclosed in 1764, the fourth year of George III's reign, but the map associated with this is faint and lacks detail. The oldest known map showing buildings within the hamlet of Coton is from 1779 (*The County of Northampton* as *surveyed and planned by the late Mr Thomas Eyre* (London: William Faden, 1780)). Although it shows a mill associated with Coton and several

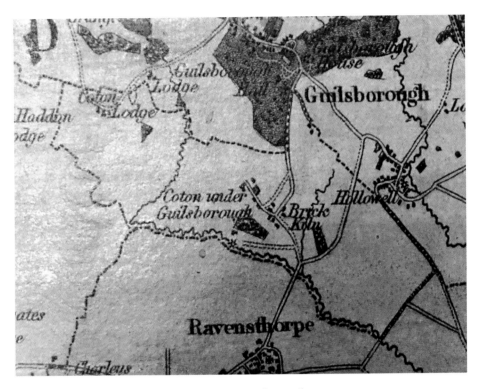

Map of the County of Northampton
(London: Greenwood, Pringle & Co., 1826)
By kind permission of Northamptonshire Record Office.

houses on both sides of the lane running through the hamlet, it does not offer detail of these buildings. The next surviving map is from 1826 (London: Greenwood, Pringle & Co., 1826) and this too shows Coton's mill (a star on the Guilsborough / Ravensthorpe border) and buildings either side of the lane. In addition, a building labelled 'Brick Kiln', is shown lying almost opposite the current Coton Manor house. Across fields to the north-west of Coton there is a building labelled Coton Lodge. A nineteenth century building with this name is currently a farmhouse in this location but earthworks suggest that a much older building existed nearby. Was this a lodge to the manor house of Coton? If so, there was a long approach to the 1662 house, but perhaps the ancient house that was slighted by the parliamentary soldiers was closer to this lodge – and to the farm that was a key feature of the manor of Coton.

Commonly, a medieval manor would have its principal dwelling house close to its farm buildings. For the manor of Coton, this farm would be Parke Farm of which a barn survives to this day on the east side of Coton's no-through lane. This farm building appears medieval in origin and takes its name from the manor's nearby old deer park. The wood to the west of the current hamlet of Coton is labelled as Old Parke or Coton Park on nineteenth century maps and this is most likely the manor's original deer park. These features may be seen on an 1839 map compiled by the tithe map maker and local Clipston man, William Bonsor. This map

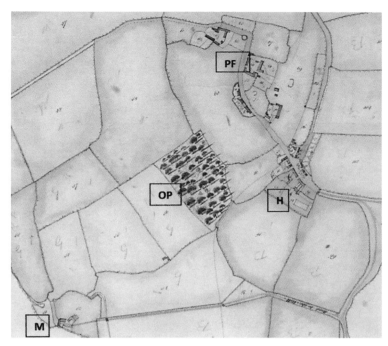

Map of Coton by William Bonsor, 1839.
By kind permission of the Northamptonshire Record Office.
(M=Mill, OP=Old Parke, H=House from 1662, PF=Parke Farm)

shows all the main components one would expect for a late medieval manor (estate), namely a large house, a mill (Coton's water-driven corn mill), a farm (Parke Farm) and a deer park (Old Parke Wood).

A manor house close to Parke Farm approached from Coton Lodge to the west may have been the building slighted during the Civil War, rather than a house built on the site of the 1662 house. Only a ninetenth century building lies near the current Parke Farm barn but this stands on land that still shows signs of earth-works with terraces at different levels. Bonsor's map shows buildings around a courtyard at the end of the lane on its west side. In Bonsor's time these were used as a farm. They no longer exist but archaeological studies have found significant amounts of medieval pottery in this area – and it's tempting to speculate that they may have been associated with the house that was at the centre of the medieval manor of Coton. Overall, there is insufficient evidence to identify the precise location of the house which was razed to the ground during the Civil War.

The 1662 Coton Manor house shown in Bonsor's 1839 map lies close to a large rectangular pond and when this map is overlaid with a current map the pond is shown to be in the same location and of the same size as in 1839. A spring close to the house feeds this pond which in turn empties into a brook that then winds its way towards the estate's water-driven corn mill. The pond is thus continually refilled with fresh water and would have been ideal as a fish pond when the house was built in 1662. Bonsor's map also shows buildings along both sides of the lane running through the hamlet. By the 1880s all the dwellings on the west side of the no-through lane have gone as seen on the First Edition Ordnance Survey map of Coton (p. 26).

At the time of the Domesday survey the Coton settlement was recorded as having nine residents and their dwellings were either side of what is today's single street running through the hamlet. In 1791 there were 17 houses in the village. By 1839 this number had reduced to 15. In the recent past the land between the lane and the valley below to the west showed signs of paddocks, platforms and closes in the form of earthworks. Unfortunately much of these earthworks have been ploughed out in recent times. Coton now lies entirely along the eastern side of this street.

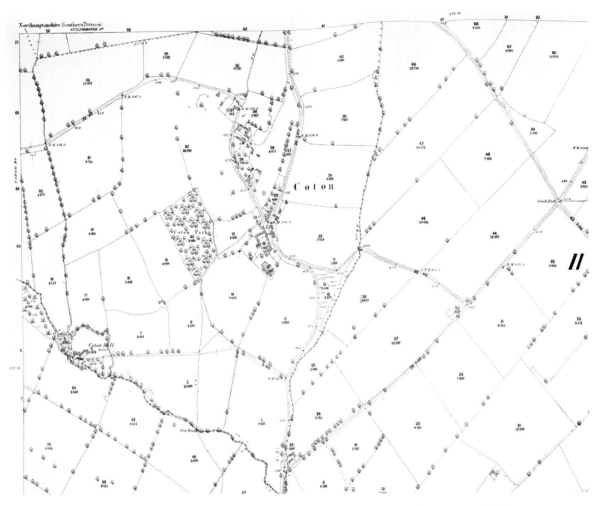

Section of the First Edition Ordnance Survey map of Coton, 1885.
By kind permission of the British Library.

At some time between the 1770s, when Lady Verney held her court at the manor, and the 1870s, the Coton Manor of 1662 became a farmhouse. By the 1871 census, John Adams farmed 206 acres of land at Coton and employed four men and two boys. Then in his early twenties, John lived at Coton with his wife, Sarah, Joseph Adams, his four-year old nephew, and Susan Seggers, a general servant aged 16 years. John was a tenant of the farm at Coton. The farm and other parts of the ancient manor of Coton were owned by the Boughton-Leighs who were related through marriage to the Verneys, Lords Willoughby de Broke. Certainly John Adams was used to life on a farm as his father, Joseph, had employed seven men when farming 260 acres at Hill Farm in Addington, Buckinhamshire (1861 census). John was Joseph's second eldest son and between 1861 and 1871 John left Addington, married and struck out on his own to farm Coton. He and Sarah had two children; both were born at Coton, John named after his father in 1872, and Elizabeth two years later. However, at the time of the 1881 census, Sarah is

Painting of Coton Farm, 1894.
By kind permission of Margaret Wilson.

listed as a widow living in Guilsborough and earning a living as a self-employed draper. At this time she shared the Guilsborough house with her children, John and Elizabeth.

Ten years later Sarah is still living at the same Guilsborough house with her son, John, who is now 18 years and listed as a chemist apprentice, and Elizabeth, a self-employed music teacher. Sarah's nephew and niece, both six-years old, also live with her. John goes on to become a well-respected chemist in Northampton. Farming was not for him and one wonders what happened to the Coton farm, his birthplace, after his father died. John's granddaughter, Margaret Wilson, now living at Cheltenham, owns a painting of Coton Manor. Painted in 1894 it carries the title 'Coton' on its frame and on the reverse, the following inscription:

A Farm House
    Coton - Nr Guilsboro'
        Northants - & birth place of my friend
           John Adams
F.G. Gill
1894

So, by at least 1894, Coton Manor became known as Coton Farm. What is now a sitting room in the 1662 part of Coton Manor house was formerly a farmhouse kitchen, as shown by the meat-hooks hanging from the ceiling. Who took over this farm when John Adams died and his wife, Sarah, moved to Guilsborough? Most likely another tenant farmer but certainly by the end of the nineteenth century Coton's history takes us to Scotland.

The 1901 census for Coton shows the residence with the highest status in the hamlet as Coton Park and this is occupied by a David Bryce Burn, aged 53, and his wife Rosia, aged 39, a married housekeeper called Harriet Davenport, and one of Harriet's daughters as a servant.

Coton's old farmhouse kitchen, now a sitting room, in the 1662 part of the manor house.

The housekeeper's husband, John, listed as a stud groom, lives with the rest of the Davenport family in the cottages next to the Coton Park residence. What stands out is that Rosia was born in Scotland as were the Davenport children, whilst David, Rosia's husband, was born in Kensington, London. This 1901 census does not list any other substantial residence within Coton and given that David Burn was a retired colonel from the 18th Hussars, it is most unlikely that he would have occupied Coton's farmhouse as it appeared in the 1894 painting. Coton Park, as listed on the 1901 census, is most likely the nineteenth–century dwelling at the end of the no-through lane in Coton close to what remains of the ancient Parke Farm, or Parke Farm itself as it became the residential dwelling it is today when it ceased to function as a farm.

Rosia was a daughter of Colonel John Anstruther-Thomson D.L., J.P. (1818 - 1904) of Charleton, Fife and of Carntyne, Lanarkshire. He was an officer in the 9th Lancers and 13th Light Dragoons, and Hon. Colonel, Fife and Forfar Imperial Yeomanry. He was a noted master of Foxhounds and was associated with the Pytchley Hunt in Northampton-shire. It is likely that Rosia would have met her future husband, David Burn, a cavalry officer, through her father's army and hunting contacts. When Rosia and David married on 20 December 1892, David was already retired and they settled in Coton, close to the Pytchley Hunt. David having a stud groom (John Davenport) supports this view. Did Rosia's father decide to support his newly married daughter and her husband by providing them with staff from his Scottish estates? John Davenport and his wife were born in England but their children were born in Scotland, and so it is likely that John, the stud groom, worked for Rosia's father in Scotland.

Another family from Scotland, the Munros, are listed on an English census for the first time in 1901 and this is also for the hamlet of Coton. The family consisted of John Murdoch (Murdo) Munro, born at Tongue in Sutherland, unmarried and aged 35, as the head of the household, his widowed mother, Elizabeth, who was 'of independent means', and a younger sister, Thomasina. Murdo Munro is described as a farmer employing two men. An advertisement in the *Northampton Mercury* of 6 July 1900 lists a M. J. Munro of Coton Grange as using a Wood's mower at this location. Was this the farm shown in the 1894 painting? Certainly the farmstead in this painting is what we know today as Coton Manor and this building was also called Coton Grange Farm in 1919 as shown in conveyance documentation for that year. Did Murdo Munro farm the land for the Burns and had the capacity to hire and fire farm-workers? If he was not so connected to the Burns, it is difficult to understand why he would move from Scotland bringing his widowed mother and his sister with him. Did this present a fresh start for the family bereft of their husband and father? Were they friends of the Davenports and decided to make the move together? What is certain is that Murdo Munro did not own Coton Grange Farm at this time: ownership still lay with the Boughton-Leigh family.

It appears that two families moved south of the border to work for the Burn newly-weds, eight Davenport family members and three people from the Munro family. The Burn couple are not listed as living in Coton on the 1911 census and neither are the Davenport family who had served them. Rosia and David had ties with Rutland and they and the Davenport family can be found in Langham, Rutland on the 1911 census. After David died in July 1915, Rosia stayed in Rutland. She married again in May 1920 and settled in Cottesmore, Oakham.

When David and Rosia moved away from Coton, so did all of the Davenports, but not the Munros. Murdo Munro was originally a game-keeper in Scotland like his father before him. However, his entry on the 1901 census when living in Coton lists him as a farmer. Would this have included game-keeping activities? One can only speculate about the nature of his work at this time but documents from 1919 still show him living in Coton with his mother and sister. His mother dies in June of that year and six months later, in December, we see his name on a conveyance as the purchaser of Coton Grange Farm. As Murdo's mother, Elizabeth, is described as 'of independent means' on the 1901 census, it seems that when she died in 1919, she left her only son with sufficient funds to purchase the freehold of Coton Grange Farm from the Boughton-Leigh family. Although Elizabeth's husband was a game keeper in his youth, in later years he became a farmer and a hotel keeper. On his death, perhaps resources from these occupations enabled her to become a widow of 'independent means'.

Certainly after his mother's death Murdo continued to farm Coton Grange and his sister kept house for him. Reports in the *Northampton Mercury* show them taking a full part in community activities, helping to raise funds for the district nursing association and other good causes, Murdo enjoying whist drives, and in 1924, playing a pivotal role in getting a directional sign for Guilsborough erected near Coton Grange to pre-empt Coton's residents being continually asked for directions by car drivers! By 1926 Murdo Munro wished to retire from farming and move to Ravensthorpe with his sister. Sadly, one year later, his sister died unexpectedly. We know from a report of her death in the *Northampton Mercury* of 11 February

1927 that 'Miss Munro had devoted her life to the care of her mother and to the domestic duties of the house of her bachelor brother'. The report continues with, 'this happy trio lived in a simple and dignified fashion for many years at Coton Grange', and 'in a quiet and unassuming way they, and especially the late Miss Munro, did far more than most people know in assisting the poor to combat their difficulties'.

So when Murdo Munro decided to sell the freehold of Coton Grange Farm in 1926, who was the purchaser and where next do we search for Coton Manor's history? America …

Elizabeth and Harold Bryant

Murdo Munro purchased Coton Grange Farm from the Boughton-Leigh family for £4,445. This was at an auction sale held at Rugby on the 16th June 1919. Thereafter, Murdo farmed the land himself with the support of two farm labourers. Eventually, the time came when he wished to retire. In 1926, when he was 73, he decided to sell the farm and move to nearby Ravensthorpe with his sister, Thomasina. He sought a purchaser who would take over Coton Grange and its surrounding farmland, including the Old Parke, and many of the animals and farm implements. The purchasers were Harold and Elizabeth Bryant, the grandparents of the current owners of Coton Manor. Harold was an English gentleman working in the United States and whilst there, married Elizabeth, a young American. So how did Harold and Elizabeth come to live at Coton?

Harold John Bryant was born in Surbiton, Surrey on 19th February 1874, to Elizabeth and Arthur Charles Bryant, a timber merchant and the brother of Wilberforce Bryant (of Bryant and May's matches). The family lived well at Oak Hill Lodge where they had a butler and several servants. The 1881 census shows Harold as the second oldest of eight children. By the time of the next census in 1891, he is seventeen and a boarder at Repton School, Derbyshire, where, like several of his brothers, he became a member of the cricket team.

He inherited his father's business acumen and as a young man became a member of Lloyds, the famous London underwriters. He came to America for the first time in 1900 as manager of a large irrigation and development project in Maxwell, New Mexico. Later, he engaged in business in Colorado Springs. It was there in 1909 with a group of Colorado associates that he became interested in south Florida and purchased an extensive amount of land in the Everglades from R. J. Bolles. In 1910 he and his associates acquired another large piece of south Florida land. This extended from West Palm Beach toward Pompano and comprised much of what is now known as the Lake Worth district in Palm Beach County.

As the head of Bryant and Greenwood and vice president of the Palm Beach Farms Company, he organised a national selling campaign that brought thousands of people from across the country into Palm Beach County to buy farms and town lots. As a founder and developer of Lake Worth he was at the forefront of those determined to create community parks and preserve the aesthetics of the lake front. He ensured commercial buildings did not encroach on residential areas. Harold was also a leading advocate of land drainage, and sugar

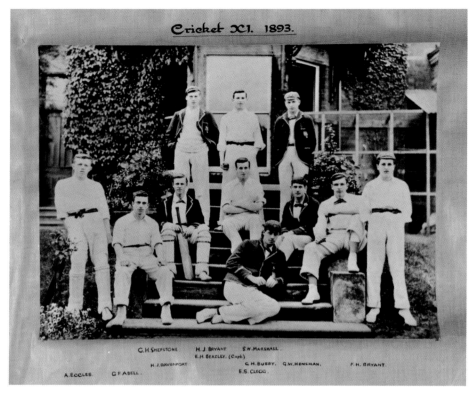

Cricket XI, 1893, Repton School, Derbyshire.
(Harold, centre back)

cane and vegetable culture in the Everglades. The period of his greatest Florida property development was from 1909 until the outbreak of World War I. In June 1913 he is described as a 'manufacturer' on the first class passenger list for the ship, 'Minnetonka', which sailed from New York to London. He was accompanied by his wife, Elizabeth, and her son and daughter from her first marriage to a Mr Gilette.

Lake Worth, Palm Beach County,
Florida.

Lake Worth: a park by the lake, 1910s.

Elizabeth was born in America in 1882 and Parker was her maiden name. She was related to the hugely wealthy Chicago-based owner of the Armour meatpacking company. The Civil War-era industrialist, Philip Danforth Armour, founded this company and moved its operations and his family to Chicago in 1865. Upon his death in 1901, his son, J. Ogden Armour, became the company's owner and president, and during his tenure Armour and Co. expanded nationwide and overseas to become the largest food products company in the United States. Elizabeth's family was also based in Chicago and very early photographs show her moving in this city's wealthy, high society circles; this included extensive travel and over-wintering in Florida. Harold either met her in Chicago or, more likely, Florida when he was actively developing land there. She had custody of her daughter, also called Elizabeth, and her son named Parker after her maiden name. Both children took Bryant as their surname on Harold and Elizabeth's marriage. Elizabeth and Harold initially settled in America but the family's 1913 journey across the Atlantic was when Europe was heading towards war. As for many families, within a year the war would separate them and Harold would miss sharing the early years of their new baby daughter's life. She was born in 1914 and named Haroldine after her father.

Considered too old for active service during WW1, Harold served as a driver with a British ambulance unit attached to the French Army from August 1917 until December 1918. He was wounded once and received the Croix de Guerre with Star. Blurry photographs capture scenes from this period of his life in western France.

Photographs taken by Harold when serving with a British
ambulance unit attached to the French Army in WW1.
(Harold is shown with coat and stick).

After the war family life revolved round homes near Chicago and in Florida. Photographs show young Haroldine enjoying the garden at the Chicago house, and in particular the grounds of the bungalow called *Mon Tresor* in Florida and its nearby beach. They show a confident, happy child, at ease in different types of surroundings.

The Bryant's house near Chicago, mid–1910s.

Haroldine in the garden.

Elizabeth in the garden.

After the war Harold continued with his work on developing Lake Worth and the Everglades area. He ensured the protection of Lake Worth's waterfront and the inclusion of community parks. Harold became increasingly interested in growing sugar cane and he owned estates in Florida which he devoted to growing this crop. He also owned a ranch in New Mexico and estates at Colorado Springs, El Paso, Colorado. The Bryant's home in Florida would continue to be enjoyed by him for vacations until his death in 1937 and, thereafter, by subsequent generations of the family.

Collecting antiques was Harold's passion, as was fox hunting. It may seem bizarre but he is credited with introducing polo into the Midwest and, as reported in a local newspaper under the heading, 'Palm Beach goes English', with initiating riding to hounds in south Florida. The first fox hunting party was held in the cattle prairies near Okeechobee City in Florida and proved popular. Fox hunting was Harold's favourite sport, although his athleticism enabled him to excel in others. Was it his love of fox hunting that drew him to return to life in England,

Harold inspecting the construction of the Florida
home, 1910s.

The family's catch of the day off
the Florida Keys.

The gardens of the Florida home.

The family at play.

or was his property development becoming overly onerous or too political? Whatever the reason, Harold and Elizabeth and their three children are all described as having their permanent address in England when they made the transatlantic crossing on the 'Aquitania' in September 1920. When Harold made this crossing on his own in September 1917 he was listed as having a permanent address in the USA but with the intention of changing this to England. So immediately after the end of WW1, Harold and Elizabeth took the major decision to move their family to England. However, Elizabeth's son, Parker, eventually lived and worked in Chicago, and the family continued to stay during the winter months at their Lake Worth home.

Where did the family live when they came to England in the 1920s? Again, transatlantic first-class passenger lists prove helpful in this respect. The list from the ship, 'Orduna', in July 1922 states that the family lived at Kelmarsh and this is their permanent residence, i.e. they are no longer primarily based in the USA. Initially, they rented the Dower House at Kelmarsh, some eleven miles from Coton. According to the next available passenger lists, by at least May 1924 they had moved seven miles closer to Coton and were renting the Grange at Spratton.

ABOVE: The Grange at Spratton, Northamptonshire, mid-1920s.

RIGHT: Elizabeth and Haroldine at the Grange, Spratton, mid-1920s.

Arguably, what brought the family to this part of England in the 1920s was Harold's desire to access the prestigious Pytchley Hunt. Its events featured regularly in publications such as *Country Life* at this time. Seeking to settle permanently in this part of England, Harold and Elizabeth searched for a property that would enable them to embrace a quintessential English country-house life-style. They bought Coton Grange Farm, animals and farm implements from Murdo Munro in March 1926 and immediately set about changing the farmhouse into a comfortable manor house.

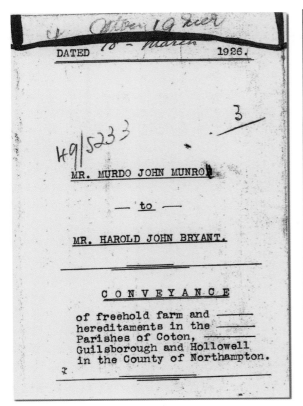

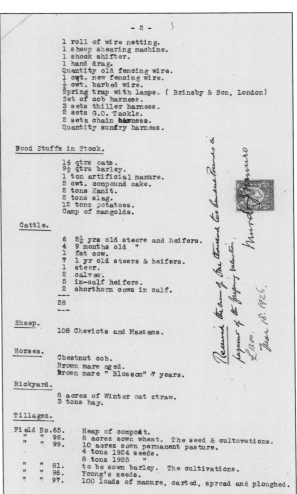

Conveyance and some of the farm implements and animals purchased by Harold Bryant from Murdo Munro in 1926.

Harold and Elizabeth sympathetically extended the farmhouse and incorporated the existing 1662 building as a south wing. They commissioned W. W. Webster, a building contractor from nearby Guilsborough, to draw up architectural plans for the substantial extension. These plans show that there were several alternative versions including ones for the south elevation with different first-floor and attic windows to what was actually built. The chosen version had the arched attic window in the 1662 south wing echoed in the extension's attic and two separate banks of windows rather than one running west to east on the first floor.

The 1662 wing had new mullioned windows inserted where the stone had eroded over the centuries and the whole of the roof was replaced. Work on the original north and east mullion windows was minimal and the 1662 indentations for metal bars and catches can still be seen here. The site must have been a hive of activity with what is now garden being used to store all the new building materials. The extension created a house that was treble the size of the 1662 farmhouse and it was ready for occupation by late 1926. Up until 1928, the new house was still called Coton Grange as shown by a newspaper report of Elizabeth presenting the prizes at Ravensthorpe's Horticultural Show in August 1927.

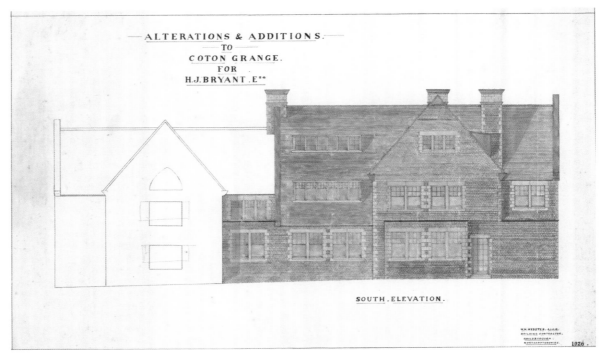

Suggested plan of the extension's south elevation, 1926.

Photograph of chosen design during construction, 1926.

Building work in progress, 1926.

When building work was nearing completion, Harold and Elizabeth turned their attention to establishing a garden. Apart from the remains of Murdo Munro's vegetable garden on the south side, the house was still surrounded by open fields. In Murdo's time, cattle had grazed right up to the original 1662 front door and had been kept away from the vegetables by a holly hedge (this hedge remains to this day). The new house stood in a commanding position overlooking Ravensthorpe's thirty acre reservoir. The ground sloped away from the house offering the potential for landscaping on different levels. There were two springs on site which fed the existing large pond on the south-west of the house and this in turn emptied into a stream flowing towards the mill.

The main fabric of the garden was established in the late 1920s and early 1930s when terraces of York stone were built around the house, pasture was converted to lawns, yew and holly hedges were planted and hundreds of trees placed on the perimeter to serve as a windbreak. This was all done with solely family enjoyment in mind and there was no inkling that it would ever be viewed by a wider public. The remains of Murdo Munro's vegetable garden with its holly hedge can be seen in a 1926 photograph taken towards the end of the building work. Harold and Elizabeth redesigned this area to create a rose garden consisting of separate beds of different roses and a pergola covered in roses and clematis at its far end. A small greenhouse was also placed against the house in this area. A white gate connected the rose garden to the rest of the garden the other side of the holly hedge.

Murdo's vegetable garden; building still in progress, 1926.

House complete with small greenhouse overlooking the Rose Garden, 1928.

The Rose Garden looking away from the house, holly hedge on the right, 1930.

White gate at the end of the holly hedge, c.1932.

Was this new garden area – and all the other landscaping activity around the house - conducted by a famous professional gardener? One might think so given the wealth and social connections of Coton's owners but evidence suggests that this was not the case. An article in the *Northampton Mercury* of 20th November 1928 refers to Mr Patience and Mr Bounds being the gardeners at Coton Manor. This article reports the Ravensthorpe wedding of Elizabeth's daughter from her first marriage. Mr Patience decorated the church with flowers in the wedding colours of pink and white and seems to have been the senior of the two gardeners. However, Mr Bounds would eventually become Head Gardener at Coton Manor and remain so until the early 1950s. William John Patrick also worked as a gardener at this time. William's son, Dennis, recalls his father taking instructions about planting directly from Harold and Elizabeth. Plants were planted at Coton Manor at the request of the couple in terms of "please plant that tree over there", "put a row of yew to form hedge here" – that is, gradually, and with no master plan in mind. No famous landscaper is known to have been involved as six acres of pasture around the south and south-west facing aspects of the extended house gradually became a garden.

The bones of the garden laid out in the late 1920s and early 1930s still exist mainly because subsequent generations have felt that this basic structure could not be improved upon. During the course of the next 90 years Coton Manor and its garden would pass through the family to the current owners, each generation lovingly refining the gardens according to fashion and personal needs. The passing years have seen the perimeter trees maturing into stately shelter belts offering welcome protection from the winds sweeping across the nearby reservoir. The rare black walnut tree planted by Harold in the centre of the stable yard in the late-1920s has grown to a height that provides shade in this area, which was changed in the late-1960s to offer plant sale and café facilities.

Time-lapse photography illustrates the rate of growth of the black walnut tree over a period of ninety years.

LEFT: Harold Bryant on his steed in 1930.
RIGHT: Harold's grandson, Ian Pasley-Tyler, outside the café / plant area in 2014.

Harold and Elizabeth left the large pond with natural edges but installed a set of steps down to the water where they remain to this day.

1926: the large pond with natural edges.

1930: the large pond with plants along its natural edges.

1926: View of the house from the field below.

The area called Goose Park where today we see flamingos roaming amongst trees and shrub roses, was left as a rough field by Elizabeth and Harold.

The York stone slabs by the 1662 front door did not extend close to the low wall and steps as they do now: there was grass either side. A sun-ray inspired bench, fashionable at the time, was installed where currently a wall fountain can be found on entering the garden.

1928: The 1662 front door garden area.

The alcove formed by the extension on the south of the house provided a sheltered area for relaxation and *al fresco* meals. The round urn shown in the photographs (opposite) appears to have been moved around the garden in the early years until finally settling where it is today, although dancing ladies aren't usually a feature now! The terracing and grass paths in this area have remained largely unaltered but the planting has changed considerably.

There was no woodland garden and only a simple water garden at this time; Murdo Munro's apple trees in the location of the current orchard and rill were retained and added to by Harold and Elizabeth. The rill was installed at this time and appeared at its best in spring when edged with narcissi. Steps leading down from the large pond area to where the rill lies were also built. They remain to this day but back then were bordered by flowering shrubs and wallflowers. Looking out from the south-facing first floor windows of the extended house in the early 1930s, one could see the grass terracing running parallel to the pond. Two large ornamental urns were at the far end of the pond and the two terraces culminated in seating areas, inviting both exploration and relaxation.

TOP LEFT: Alcove garden with grass and round urn, c.1930.

TOP RIGHT: Alcove garden: relaxation and *al fresco* eating.

LEFT: Round urn in the middle of the grass terrace.

LEFT: Rill created in the late-1920s.

TOP RIGHT: Steps leading from large pond to the orchard and rill area, late-1920s.

BOTTOM RIGHT: View from the south-facing first floor windows, early-1930s.

Life settled into one where Harold participated regularly in the Pytchley Hunt and Coton Manor became a much favoured venue for social events and family gatherings. Each Christmas the Bryants gave a Christmas tree and tea party for the children of Ravensthorpe, Coton and Teeton and as the years went by, Haroldine organised dances and fund-raising events.

Harold and Elizabeth's love of travel saw them regularly over-wintering at their Florida home and taking Haroldine on exotic trips. She kept some postcards of the places she visited with her parents

RAVENSTHORPE

THE SCHOOL CHILDREN of Ravensthorpe, Coton, and Teeton were entertained to the usual Christmas tree and tea which has now for several years past been given them by Mr. and Mrs. Harold Bryant and their daughter, Miss Haroldine, of Coton Manor. A Christmas tree, loaded with presents and decorations had been prepared, and after a sumptuos tea and carol singing, the children had a royal time. The Vicar expressed the gratitude of the children and workers to the family of Coton Manor.

Northampton Mercury, 4 January 1935.

and these show that her passion for plants was acquired from an early age. It is also clear that father and daughter were particularly close.

1930s: Happy Holidays !

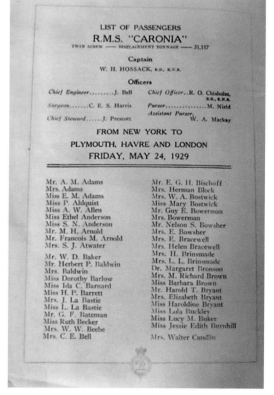

Transatlantic sailing.

Haroldine as Hawaiian
maiden.

Harold and Haroldine giving their Roman verdict.

Pan American sea-plane.

Haroldine rowing off
Sorrento.

Light aircraft travel across the Midwest.

Harold and Haroldine shared a love of hunting but in 1930 when Haroldine was just 16 years of age, she had a serious riding accident. Her pelvis was broken. It took more than a year for her to recover sufficiently to be seen out and about and three years before she could hunt again. Family photographs show Haroldine recovering in the Rose Garden, either on crutches or relaxing on a sun-lounger. The same area would be altered by her some two decades later when she inherited Coton Manor and became a knowledgeable plantswoman. In the latter part of 1931, Haroldine spent some time in Florence and Paris, combining study with recuperation.

HUNTING FIELD ACCIDENT.

Horse Rolls on Miss Haroldine Bryant.

Rolled upon by her horse after it had reared and thrown her, a young follower of the Pytchley Hounds was badly injured towards the close of the day's run.

She was Miss Haroldine Bryant, the 16-year-old daughter of Mr. and Mrs. Harold Bryant, of Coton Manor, Guilsborough.

Her brother, Mr. A. P. Bryant, and other hunting people carried her on a hurdle to Loddington Hall, where she was seen by Dr. Whiting.

Later the Market Harborough ambulance was called, and she was taken home to Guilsborough.

TOP LEFT: Harold and Haroldine. *BOTTOM LEFT:* Haroldine's riding accident.
RIGHT: Haroldine recovering in the Rose Garden.

By 1932 Haroldine is reported in newspapers as taking a leading role again in the fund raising events held at Coton Manor. Bridge parties at the Manor were used to raise funds for various hospitals, and each summer the Manor's garden was given over to charitable fete activities. A report of a fete held at the Manor in 1932 says that 'Miss Haroldine Bryant had a stall of fancy goods, many of which she had made herself … indeed during the early part of the afternoon she was seen unashamedly knitting a white woolly sweater, which she later put up for sale! … The other daughter of the house, now Mrs Rathbone, was engaged in raffling a book'. The Ravensthorpe fete of 1934 was held at Coton Manor to raise funds for Northampton General Hospital and coincided with Elizabeth's son, Parker, from her first marriage, coming back to Coton after living in America for three years. An account in the *Mercury and Herald* captures the family and friends in the Manor's garden.

AT RAVENSTHORPE FETE

County supporters of Ravensthorpe Village Fete, held at Coton Manor, on Tuesday. Left to right:—Standing: Major Harold Bryant, Captain Rathbone, Lord Erskine of Restormel, Mrs. Parker Bryant, Mrs. Cecil Bates, Lady Erskine and Mr. Parker Bryant. Seated: Miss Lila Fortescue, Miss Louise Fermor-Hesketh (holding black dog), Mrs. Bryant (behind), Mrs. Lorents Rathbone, Master Adrian Garnet, the Hon. Mrs. Fortescue, and (seated below) Miss Haroldine Bryant.

Mercury and Herald, 10 August 1934.

Haroldine made her debut (came out) in 1933, being presented by her mother. In May 1934 she left England for Malta, where she intended to pay a long visit to her sister whose husband, Captain Rathbone, served in the Rifle Brigade there. It is understood that Haroldine met her future husband at this time. Certainly in April 1938 her engagement to Lieutenant Henry Pasley-Tyler, who served in the Royal Navy in Malta, was announced in newspapers.

WEDDING at Ravensthorpe of Miss Haroldine Bryant, of Coton Manor, and Lieutenant H. P. Tyler, R.N. On the left are the bride and bridegroom, and on right the bridemaids and best man—Miss Dorothy Gage, Lieutenant A. Gordon-Lennox, R.N., Miss Kitty Fullerton, and Susan Senior.

RAVENSTHORPE

THE WEDDING of Miss Haroldine Bryant to Lieutenant Henry Pasley-Tyler, R.N., which took place on Saturday last, was an occasion for much rejoicing in the village. The local band of ringers marked the event by ringing peals, and in the evening a socal and dance was given to the people of Ravensthorpe and Coton by Mrs. Bryant. While refreshments were being served, Mrs. Bryant, accompanied by her son, Mr. Parker Bryant, and the Comte de Dane, joined the party. They were loudly cheered and thanked by the Vicar, the Rev. T. W. Long. During the evening a telegram was received from the bride and bridegroom wishing the parishioners a happy evening and also expressing their gratitude for the wedding presents sent by the villagers and children.

Mercury and Herald, 14 May 1938.

Mercury and Herald, 20 May 1938.

Their marriage took place on the 14th May that year at St. Denys Church, Ravensthorpe, followed by a reception at Coton Manor. The church was decorated with spring flowers, almost entirely grown within the Manor's gardens. The colour theme was yellow and Mr Kenny, the butler, decorated the house. Haroldine and Henry honeymooned in Italy, after which they paid a flying visit to Coton before leaving to live in Malta where Henry still served. So the two sisters were reunited, albeit for the time being, many miles from Coton.

Haroldine was not given away by her father at her marriage. Just one year before, on 11 May 1937 and aged just 63 years, Harold suffered a fatal heart attack whilst staying at 44 York Terrace, Marylebone, London. He had gone from Coton to London in preparation for attending the coronation of George VI on the 12th May. During the previous year he regularly hunted with the Pytchley and his death came as a great shock. It was widely reported on both sides of the Atlantic. In honour of his work associated with the founding and development of Lake Worth, the city commission designated the lake-front park south of Lake Avenue and east of R Street as 'Harold J. Bryant Park'. After Harold's death Elizabeth continued to spend the winter months in Florida but otherwise lived at Coton for another ten years. She died aged 65 years on 9 January 1947 at a nearby nursing home with her son-in-law, Henry Pasley-Tyler, in attendance.

Harold and Elizabeth's marriage was full of vibrant experiences. They traversed the world when intercontinental travel was a rarity and yet made a quiet corner of Northamptonshire their main home. They turned Coton Grange Farm into a quintessential English country manor and laid the bones of a six acre garden that remain to this day. Recently, when Harold's grandson, Ian Pasley-Tyler, came to search Coton Manor's attic for items relating to the early history of the house, he came across a small box of dried flowers labelled 'Flowers on altar of Elizabeth's and Harold's wedding'. How poignant that this has stayed hidden at Coton Manor whilst a further two generations of the family have continued to occupy and care for the house and garden that Harold and Elizabeth so clearly loved.

Box lid states: 'Flowers on altar of Elizabeth's and Harold's wedding'.

Haroldine as a young gardener.

Haroldine and the Commander

In June 1938, and after their honeymoon near Lake Garda, Henry and Haroldine Pasley-Tyler returned to Malta where Henry was stationed in the Royal Navy. Like many young couples at this time, the early years of their marriage were shaped by WW2 and its aftermath. It would be another twelve years before they would settle at Coton Manor.

Henry and Haroldine in Malta and their naval quarters, late-1930s.

Henry's father was Major Alfred Herbert Tyler. He served in the Royal Engineers and was killed in action on the 11th November 1914 when allied forces retook Ypres from the Germans. Born 28 May 1911, Henry was but three years old when his father was killed. Henry's grandfather was Sir Henry Whatley Tyler (1827 - 1908). Sir Henry had a distinguished career which included serving as an MP. He was a British Inspector of Railways for more than twenty years, and his expertise was called upon not only in the UK but also in various locations in Europe. In 1866 he was sent to inspect the railway systems of France and Italy in order to determine how best to transfer mail destined for India from northern France to the Italian port of Brindisi. On his recommendation the route was accepted. In 1867 he investigated London's water supply following an outbreak of cholera. His report helped confirm that cholera was water-borne rather than by the air. In 1868 he spent two periods of leave building the first railway in Greece from Athens to Piraeus. He went to America to inspect the Erie for British investors, to Canada as a consultant for the Trans Canadian Railway system, and in 1875 and 1876 he was a member of the abortive Channel Tunnel Commission. In later life, his interest in homeopathy led him to contribute large sums of money for the expansion of the London Homeopathic Hospital.

Sir Henry married the daughter of General Sir Charles Pasley. When the continuation of the Pasley name was in doubt, it was suggested that one of sons in the subsequent generations of the Tyler side of the family should be called Pasley-Tyler. This is why Haroldine's husband was called Henry Pasley-Tyler whilst his brothers only carried the Tyler surname. Like the Tylers, the Pasley side of the family also had members who had notable careers. One naval ancestor distinguished himself with a bold rescue of a foreign princess. It is worth telling here for its uniqueness – and indication of the indomitable spirit running through the Pasley-Tyler family. During the mid-1860s, Princess Salme, a sister of successive Sultans of the island of Zanzibar, became friendly with a young German businessman, Heinrich Ruete. The flat roof of his house in the old capital, Stone Town, was a little lower than hers, so she could see into the rooms and observe his dinner parties at which European men sat beside European women. By contrast, Muslim women on Zanzibar were fully veiled and covered when they went out, and broke the law simply by speaking to male strangers. However, even as a little girl, Princess Salme had shown her fearless spirit by climbing palm trees, learning to shoot and ride, as well as to read and write, all rare attainments for royal women. Perhaps her self-confidence, and the ease with which she and the 30-year-old German entrepreneur were able to meet unobserved on her roof, led her to underrate the possibility of discovery. The princess fell in love with Heinrich and became pregnant. It was a tragic situation, since under sharia law the appropriate punishment for this liaison was that both lovers should be killed, with Princess Salme being stoned to death.

Heinrich Ruete escaped, but when the 22-year-old princess tried to stowaway on one of the ships owned by her lover's company, she was caught and placed under house arrest in July 1866. Captain T. M. S. Pasley, a senior officer in the Royal Navy's East African Anti-Slave Trade Squadron, was told in secrecy by the British Consul's wife that if Princess Salme remained on the island, she would be put to death. The Consul had ruled out interfering in the private affairs of Zanzibar's royal family. Nevertheless, Captain Pasley lost no time in devising a plan for rescuing the princess. A religious festival was due to take place that required Muslims to go down to the beach to wash. So, on the day itself – August 26, 1866 – a ship's cutter, manned by sailors from Pasley's cruiser, HMS Highflyer anchored in Zanzibar's harbour, was dispatched to the shore to collect the princess and her servants from a rendezvous point. Pasley intended to come in close to the shore in the captain's gig [a smaller ship's boat] to be on hand in case fighting broke out. The plan was successful and Pasley conveyed the princess to Aden in his ship where she received Christian instruction and married Ruete. She remained in contact with Captain Pasley throughout his life.

Princess Salme, *c.*1860s.

Although not rescuing any exotic foreign princesses in his time, Henry Pasley-Tyler had a very successful naval career! He also had an interest in construction (arguably inherited from the Sir Henry Whatley Tyler side of the family) which found an outlet in the garden at Coton Manor across the years. From being a naval cadet in 1929, Henry progressed through the ranks to become a Commander in 1946. He specialized in both visual signalling and wireless telegraphy. A photograph taken aboard ship when he was a lieutenant based in Malta reveals an engaging smile that characterises his confidence and outgoing personality.

Henry Pasley-Tyler, 1930s. (Second row, fourth from right.)

Henry was stationed at various locations around the world during the war years. For a time he was based in England, and Haroldine and he lived at Liphook, Hampshire. By 1940 Haroldine was expecting their first child and she stayed with her mother at Coton during her confinement. A baby boy, Ian, was born 1 November 1940 at Barratt Maternity Home in Northampton. Five years later, Ian would be joined by a brother, Robert, who was also born at the same maternity home – but much would happen to the family before that event.

Henry and Haroldine with baby Ian (*b*.01.11.40), March 1941.
(Coton Manor, between the house and the stable yard.)

Photographs taken during Haroldine's visits to Coton between 1942 and 1943 show the Rose Garden with eight rectangular rose beds, each filled with one particular variety, central and perimeter grass pathways, a stone birdbath set in a circular depression, and a rose-covered pergola at the far end. Although there was a yew hedge with an opening leading through to what is now the Woodland Garden, it would take several more years before the opening would grow into an archway. The greenhouse attached to the house and stretching out into the Rose Garden had not yet been replaced by the Loggia. The pond was fenced off and it still had its rough, natural edges. A path tracked across the lawn in front of the house.

View of the Rose Garden and the Holly Hedge Border, *c.*1940s.

Ian in the Rose Garden with a view of its pergola and the greenhouse, *c.*1943.

House with track across the lawn, and the pond with fence and rough edges, *c.*1943.

Haroldine and Ian visiting Coton on his
seventh birthday, 01.11.1947.
(Note the wisteria being trained to form an umbrella shape, and
the repaired stonework from the 1920s.)

Henry's knowledge and experience of wireless communications led him to become a member of the British naval mission at the Pentagon, Washington, U.S.A. in 1947. He served as a communications adviser for some three years during which time Haroldine was either staying with him in Washington or living at Liphook in Hampshire with their two sons, Ian and Robert. Haroldine's mother, Elizabeth Bryant, died in January, 1947 and in April 1948 Haroldine and the two boys sailed on the Queen Mary from Southampton to New York to be reunited with Henry. The family remained in Washington for the next two years, and occasionally holidayed at Harold and Elizabeth Bryant's old Palm Beach home.

In 1950 Henry left the British naval mission in Washington, the family returned to England, and their life together at Coton Manor began. Henry was 38 and on the 1st July that same year joined Elliott Automation Ltd. in Borehamwood, Hertfordshire.

His naval background in wireless communications and his experience with the British naval mission were extremely useful to the company. Formed in 1804 by William Elliott in London and known as Elliott Brothers, the company initially consisted of electrical and mechanical engineers. During the early 1900s it developed specialities in ships' logs, and all kinds of speed indicators and telegraph apparatus. Throughout WW2 the company manufactured parts for armaments but in 1946 it established research laboratories at Borehamwood for the development of computers and flight automation equipment. When Henry joined the company in 1950, it was in the throes of directing more of its activities towards computing. The first Elliott 152 computer was produced that year. Successive take overs by English Electric and then GEC during the 1960s created several subsidiary companies. However, the real-time computer part of Elliott Automation remained in the original Borehamwood research laboratories until the 1990s.

Henry was tasked with liaising between Elliotts and the Admiralty at a time when internal politics threatened to disrupt the whole company. By mid-1952 Henry had gained the confidence of the research staff and henceforward became an effective and respected top-level negotiator in Borehamwood's research contracts, especially those involving the Ministry of Defence. He became the senior man at Borehamwood and had overall authority for the company's military business. Prince Philip visited the Borehamwood laboratories on 17 May 1963; Henry was awarded a CBE for Services to Export in 1968.

Elliott's stand at the Farnborough Show, 1964.

Generally, Henry stayed at the family's London home during the week and returned to Coton Manor at the weekends. When the family moved into the Manor in the spring of 1950, they found a great deal needed their attention. During the war years Coton's garden was only nominally cared for by an Italian prisoner of war and this, combined with Elizabeth's failing health and her death in 1947, led to the garden falling into a state of neglect. With Henry's need to have all things 'ship-shape', a plan of action was put in place. With two young sons who could be cajoled into assisting him, gardeners keen to be employed in the post-war years, and Haroldine's increasing interest in plants, it was 'all hands on deck'. Reclamation, replanting and much new development work took place in the 1950s and 1960s. When Henry returned to Coton from Borehamwood for the weekend, he immersed himself in gardening and construction activities. Commander Henry Pasley-Tyler, or 'The Commander', as those working at Coton called him through both respect and affection, set a standard of garden maintenance that family members recall was often at odds with Haroldine's more relaxed style of gardening! But it all worked … and gradually, Coton's garden came back to life within the surviving basic structure laid out by Haroldine's parents in the late 1920s.

Henry and Ian, 1950, and the same area, 2014.
(Note the presence of a pergola on the 'poop deck' in 1950; Henry, with the assistance of Dennis Patrick, inserted the curved steps during the 1960s.)

Ian and dog by the Holly Hedge Border, 1950.
(Note there are no plants on the top of the low wall of the terrace as there are today.)

Holly Hedge Terrace and the pergola system beyond, clothed in roses.

Although as Coton's owners, Haroldine and Henry were the driving force in all of the gardening activity, what was achieved was due to – and continues to be – a huge team effort. When Haroldine and Henry took over Coton in 1950 they were assisted by Head Gardener, Mr. Ralph Endicott. He had previously worked at Coton during Harold and Elizabeth's time as did Mr Ray Butlin who had carpentry skills and could turn his hand to most DIY activities. In 1953 they were joined by Dennis Patrick, aged 15 and straight from school. Dennis's father had also worked in the gardens when

Mr. Endicott, c.1940s.

Harold and Elizabeth owned Coton. Mr George Gurney joined the team, more as a handyman than as a gardener, as there was a considerable amount of construction work needed in the garden to implement the plans of Henry and Haroldine.

Within a year of moving into Coton Manor, the couple placed an advertisement in the *Herald and Mercury*; it offered Khaki Campbell ducks for sale to make space for young stock. The following year another advertisement offered Aylesbury duck egg settings for sale together with ornamental ducks; production was in full swing at the Manor.

The selling of ducks in full swing.
(*Mercury and Herald*, May, 1952.)

Henry and Haroldine went into the rearing and selling of chickens, turkeys and ducklings and this venture continued until the mid-1960s. Where now we see a brick potting shed in the Plant Nursery, there was a large, deep-litter poultry house. Breeding took place throughout the year to capitalize on out-of-season sales. Some sixty years on, Haroldine and Henry's son, Ian, still remembers how busy Mondays could get in the 1950s as the birds were processed for sale: they had to be killed, plucked, bled, waxed to remove pin feathers, dressed, and then a significant number were frozen. Haroldine and anyone working at Coton at this time were all hands-on in these activities.

Pullets behind the white poultry house,
1959.

The same area, 2014:
'rearing' of a different kind.
(By kind permission of Caroline Tait.)

Some of the first freezers to exist in England were brought over from the U.S.A. for storing the frozen birds. The area in the Café where people now order their refreshments was lined and turned into a large walk-in freezer. Furthermore, the walled garden area was given over to the growing of soft fruit, mainly strawberries and raspberries. Some of these fruits were also frozen and by 1952 Coton Manor, then known as Coton Hall Manor, was advertising a range of 'quick frozen foods'.

COTON MANOR
QUICK FROZEN FOODS

The simple solution to
your   food   problem

TURKEYS, CHICKENS, DUCKLINGS,
VEGETABLES AND SOFT FRUIT

Always available at short
notice all the year round.
Everything grown on the
farm, hand prepared and
ready to cook

PERFECT QUALITY AT REASONABLE
PRICES. —   Price list from

COTON HALL MANOR
TELEPHONE GUILSBOROUGH 219.

Coton: poultry farm and market garden.
(*Herald and Mercury*, 21 March, 1952.)

Haroldine went to great lengths to locate buyers for the Manor's produce. Her old Buick car was loaded with frozen poultry and fruit which she then drove to various Oxford and Cambridge colleges. Top London hotels were also targeted, including the Connaught. One can only imagine how cold Haroldine became on those journeys. It wasn't long before she got Ray Butlin (handyman at Coton Manor and the village's carpenter) to build a screen between her and the frozen goods in the back of the car.

In 1955 Henry embarked on several construction projects. Sons, Ian and Robert, and Dennis Patrick were key assistants; Mr Endicott still had more of a focus on the horticultural side of the garden. The greenhouse attached to the Manor was converted into an entrance area for a new, long loggia roofed with Collyweston stone. This provided a welcome summer reception area overlooking the Rose Garden. It quickly became more useful than the alcove outside the dining room which had been used by Harold and Elizabeth for *al fresco* meals. A few years later, this alcove had its windows greatly enlarged and a raised area was put beneath them, all of which enabled easy access to and from the dining room. The new Loggia was furnished with comfortable chairs around a fireplace and was decorated with tables topped with tiles from Haroldine's collections. Like her father, Haroldine loved hunting for decorated stoneware and porcelain. The table one now sees on being greeted at Garden School events in the Loggia's entrance area is covered with some of Haroldine's treasured tiles. Indeed, the Loggia itself is now given over to Garden School events – but they were still to come in the next generation of the family.

The Loggia was built a year after the birth of Henrietta, a sister for Ian and Robert. Family photographs show her enjoying the sheltered space outside the Loggia with her older brothers and her nurse. This area was still devoted to roses but within new radially arranged beds rather than the old rectangular ones. The round urn that had stood in the far corner of this garden was repositioned at the centre of the new beds. The hybrid tea roses were replaced by herbaceous peonies and shrub roses, and all was counterpointed by a shapely bed of mostly grey- and silver-foliaged plants. The stone ornament set in a circular depression was turned into a small pond and fountain by the loggia doors. Raised beds against this garden's perimeter stone wall provided shelter for *Choisya ternata*, *Abutilon vitifolium*, *Clerodendrum trichotomum* and the beautiful Blue Lagoon form of *Clematis macropetala*.

Loggia under construction, 1955.

New Rose Garden layout, 1955.

ABOVE: Henrietta with her brothers and her
nurse outside the new Loggia.

Rose Garden in full bloom, 1956.

Photographs from 1955 show the main pond with natural, rough edges, and wildfowl roaming this area of the garden. Ian recalls that every summer, without fail, the pond would quickly turn to a bright green soup, thanks to a healthy colony of algae. Chemical treatments were tried to no avail, so black East Indies ducks were brought in. Their appetite proved insatiable and the pond soon assumed its required crystal clarity. Henry and Haroldine were then unable to resist introducing more waterfowl. This marked the start of the avicultural era at Coton Manor and it is from this time that the number and variety of birds kept at the Manor continually increased until the late 1970s. Henry decided to edge the pond with stone and create islands to form safe breeding sites. A seating area reached by steps was carved out of the banking, and a bench and table, both painted white, were installed to provide a place of relaxation from which to admire the antics of the ducks. Later, when a pink Japanese flowering cherry tree (*Prunus kanzan*) was planted near this spot, there were glorious multiple pink reflections on the water. When this tree succumbed to old age in 1994, the next generation of the Pasley-Tyler family replaced it with a white flowering variety. Now, during spring, its blossoms appear as a snowfall underneath the tree and on the water.

Black East Indies ducks and signets walking on the pond's ice, 1955.

Stone edges around the pond in place by 1959.

The outside area where plants are now sold and people enjoy the Café's refreshments was still very much a stable yard until 1969. On the opposite side, where currently a few cars may park on open days, a hedge with walkway enclosed an area to the left of the Manor's door. Only a small section of this hedge remains today and has been turned into topiary balls.

Dennis Patrick remembers Henry making forays to the auctions at Crowthers in London during the 1960s. He was seeking architectural pieces that would add interest to the garden. With the weight of the stone and metal objects in the back of an old land rover, it's a wonder the tyres got Henry home. Several pieces were purchased including a small fountain. Dennis installed this against the wall one passes on entering the garden through the wooden gate attached to the house. Previously, this area had held a sunburst-designed bench. This bench was painted white and moved to an alcove containing a table in the holly bush overlooking the

Henry by the *Prunus kanzan* and the pond, 1959.

The *Prunus kanzan* in full flower, 1960.

pond and main lawn. A large carved clock-face was sunk into the pathway to the left of the Manor's front door but was later moved to be closer to the fountain by the garden gate. It may now be seen partly covered by a large metal container filled with spring bulbs and other plants throughout the year.

Dennis Patrick and the bench that was moved from the stone wall where he installed the fountain over fifty years ago.

Pride of place must go to the two Italian well-heads, one of which also came from Crowthers' auction rooms. This particular one was positioned in the shade of the towering chestnut tree. In high summer this is now a favourite area from which to admire the pond, house and acacia border. In Haroldine's time this border was known as 'the little border', and was devoted to a backdrop of acacia trees and perennials. Angelica, sweet rocket, foxgloves, echinops and onopordon were planted in front of the trees. Close to the border's edge with the main lawn, hellebores, euphorbias and eryngiums added interest for most of the year.

Dennis Patrick by the well-head under the chestnut tree.

The other well-head came from land in Borehamwood near the site of Elliott Automation where Henry worked. It replaced the round urn positioned at the centre of the Rose Garden's four quadrant beds in the mid-1950s. This well-head is certainly inspired by Renaissance art. Its sides are composed of alternating designs of men chanting from a scroll and from a book. These designs are taken from marble sculptures known as the Cantoria created by Luca della Robbia in 1431-38 for the Cathedral of Santa Maria del Fiore in Florence. They are considered one of the masterpieces of the early Florentine Renaissance and are now preserved in the Museo dell'Opera del Duomo. Florence was very popular with wealthy Americans and British aristocrats in the beginning of the twentieth century. They either stayed there throughout the winter months, or made new homes from the old villas on the surrounding hills, many of which had fallen into disrepair. A significant number of architectural pieces in Florence were bought and shipped back to Britain and America at this time. It is more than likely that this is how the Rubbio-inspired well-head came to London before it eventually found its way to Coton via Henry and his land rover.

Coton's Florentine well-head in the Rose Garden.

Cantoria by Luca della Robbia, 1431–38, Museo dell'Opera del Duomo, Florence.

At the top of the Water Garden lying across a rivulet there is a small section of stone that looks like part of an old mullioned window. Dennis recalls it being in this position when he joined Coton in 1953. So was it placed there during Coton's rebuilding in 1662 or did Harold and Elizabeth install it when they came in 1926? Is it a remnant of pre-1662 Coton Manor, a fragment of Holdenby's glory days or did it come from nearby Northampton Castle which was also demolished and had its stone used in various locations? The sleuthing continues - but look for this piece when next you visit the water garden and form your own opinions of its age and source ...

Architectural remains in the Water Garden.

Henry (the Commander) retired from Elliotts at the end of the 1960s. This marked an increase in the tempo of developments at Coton Manor. There was an immediate rise in the number and type of birds kept at Coton. Henry and Haroldine shared a love of nature in its various forms and that was particularly reflected in their ownership of different types of birds, some of which had the run of the garden around the house. The expansion of bird life called for additional enclosures, pools and waterways together with low unobtrusive fencing to protect the plant life. These enclosures were mainly positioned where now we see wildfowl roaming freely amongst flamingos in parkland below the house. The original rill installed by Harold and Elizabeth in the 1920s was the same length as the version we see today by the Old Orchard. However, in Elizabeth's time the rill had three square ponds, each six by eight feet, positioned at either end of the rill and at its mid-point. The top pond contained a lead cherub fountain – the same fountain that we see today in the centre of the Rose Garden's pond. Henry swept this arrangement away. Two new ponds were created in this area, one slightly higher up the orchard slope than the other, and both were fenced around to house some of the wildfowl. A rill feature would be reinstated here by the next generation of the family in the 1990s.

One of Henry's ponds at the top of the Old Orchard, c.1960s.

Elegant demoiselle cranes, peacocks, many species of duck, geese of various kinds, rare black-necked swans, golden pheasants, macaws, and Chilean and Caribbean flamingos, the latter with bright pink plumage, enjoyed the Manor's garden. At one point a number of macaws were flying everywhere, including throughout the bluebell wood; they all had to be locked up at night – no easy task!

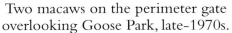

Two macaws on the perimeter gate overlooking Goose Park, late-1970s.

A demoiselle crane and black-neck swans with their signets, late-1970s.

The flamingo population at Coton soared to 20 when Henry joined forces with Peter Scott, who had managed to import a large flock of flamingos from the Bahamas for his own breeding programme at Slimbridge. In a photograph of this time, the pink of the Japanese flowering cherry in full flower melds with the pink of the Caribbean flamingos in the pond.

Caribbean flamingos roaming freely near the Manor House during the time of Haroldine and Henry.

This was a scene capable of stopping people in their tracks – and by 1969 there were rather more people than before walking around the pond. This was because Henry and Haroldine decided to open the garden to the public that year, a huge commitment made necessary by the soaring costs of upkeep and Henry's retirement.

The Manor's garden reflected Haroldine's expertise as a knowledgeable plantswoman with an excellent eye for harmony in colour and form. Now that the garden was open to the public, it became increasingly important to provide interest through the seasons. In 1971, the field below the garden was planted with a scattering of trees and became known as Goose Park. Two parallel mixed borders were created at the top section of this park. They were planted with trees, shrubs and herbaceous perennials with an accent on colour and interest in late summer and autumn. Initially, the soil here was heavy clay but Haroldine and Henry added huge quantities of leaf mould and bonfire ash. These borders were the last ones to be created in Haroldine's time at Coton. The five acre Bluebell Wood beyond Goose Park then consisted of beech and larch trees. Although accessible by visitors when the garden was open, the wood did not draw people in the numbers that it does today.

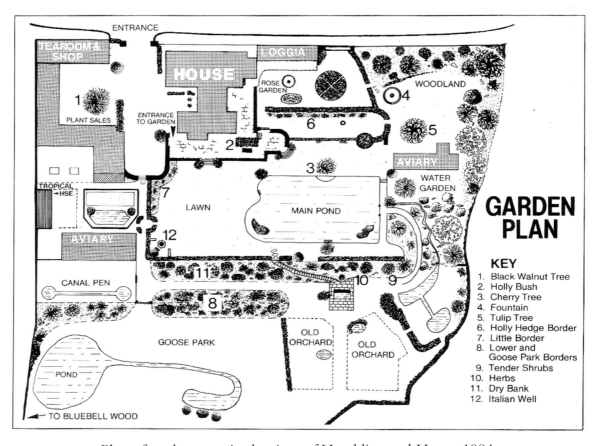

Plan of garden areas in the time of Haroldine and Henry, 1984.

The border running along the holly hedge facing the pond was a conventional herbaceous border, at its best in June and July. It provided a symphony of soft colours – many blues and whites with some yellows and a few deeper tones of red – from summer through to early autumn. Fine old peonies, several varieties of aconitum, phlox, astrantias, monarda, herbaceous clematis, sedums and fuchias were planted here. The Woodland Garden existed but on a much smaller scale than we see today and with very few snowdrops. It was planted with trilliums and epimediums, Solomon's seal and the related *Smilacina racemosa*, hostas, and the double-flowered form of the white *Sanguisorba canadensis*. All luxuriated in the dappled shade provided by an assortment of mature trees. Most of these were planted in the late 1920s when the garden was first created by Haroldine's parents, Harold and Elizabeth Bryant.

The woodland area merged into the Water Garden, at the top of which Henry positioned a long aviary of Quaker Parakeets. Any pergola supports from the Bryants' time in this area were removed. Henry decided to enlarge the Water Garden and additional pools and rivulets were created. Ferns flourished in the damp conditions. Hostas, astilbes, primulas, sweet-scented azaleas and the pink-flowered umbrella plant, *Peltiphyllum peltatum*, put on a good show in spring. They were joined by the 'bog arum', *Lysichitum americanum*, and the striking *Iris foetidissima* 'Variegata'. Henry created a long pool towards the bottom of the water garden area. This joined to a new round pool at the lowest point. The latter was formed from a sunken grassed area in the middle of which was an unusual, very pretty weeping willow with smaller than normal leaves. A table encircled the tree and it was a pleasant place to sit. When Henry swept this all away, he added a small wooden shelter near the round pool (not the current summer house).

Looking down the Water Garden with azaleas in flower, 1980s.

Coming from the Water Garden towards the old orchard, one would pass a bank of tender shrubs, many from Australasia. A little further on, this bank became a herb border and extended beyond the steps leading down from the main pond. This dry area of the bank was planted with shrub and old roses, mainly pink and white varieties, all of which were interspersed with irises, hostas, lilacs, mock oranges and *Helleborus foetidus*. A little further on, one came to the top of Goose Park where Henry and Haroldine could often be seen with their favourite birds.

The greenhouse set against the stone wall in the Walled Garden was used to create an illusion of the tropics. Inside, succulents, cacti, plumbagoes, palms, passion flowers, mimosas and abutilons vied for attention with some sixty different kinds of pelargoniums, many of which were scented–leaved varieties. Henry and his assistants built a low stone wall dividing the interior in two. The wall ran the entire length of the greenhouse. At its mid-point, the wall curved in towards the back wall where there was a fountain.

Henry, Haroldine, Emma the macaw, and free-range flamingos in Goose Park, c.1970s.

The back of the low wall was filled with soil to create two long raised beds. The fountain fed a pool beneath it, which in turn fed another pool at floor level. As described in the following chapter, this greenhouse underwent massive changes after Henry and Haroldine died. Today, the fountain can be seen positioned outside the greenhouse to the left of the archway as one leaves the walled garden. This archway now leads to the plant storage and poly-tunnel area; up until 1991, there were only compost heaps here. People remember this greenhouse from Haroldine's and Henry's time as an exotic space during summer, full of wonderful scents, colours and the gentle sound of water trickling from the fountain. It was known as the tropical house, although the temperatures reached inside never lived up to that description. This house had to be dual purpose: it was decorative during the summer when open to visitors, but very utilitarian in winter when it had to house all of Coton's tender plants. Not an inch of space was unused.

When Henry was asked by a reporter how the high standard of Coton's garden was achieved and maintained, he replied, 'By iron self-discipline'. With so many plant features to tend, birds to look after, many with special feeding requirements, and so much grass to mow, self-discipline was a prerequisite. Between spring and autumn, and at least once a week, over a mile of lawn edgings were trimmed with a battery-powered lawn edger. The rough grass was cut with one or other of the Pasley-Tylers' two Wheel-Horse lawn tractors, which were also used for other tasks when their trailers were attached. The lawns were cut with conventional lawnmowers. Lawns and their care became a particular interest for Henry, an interest that was sustained into old age, even when his son and daughter-in-law took over the care of the garden in 1991.

It was once the garden opened to the public that Henry and Haroldine considered adding to Coton's attractions by introducing other types of animals. This reflected what was happening elsewhere: the 1960s and 1970s saw an increase in country estates keeping a variety of animals with the aim of increasing their visitor numbers. In the early 1970s Henry imported two

Coton's two sealions, mid-1970s.

sealions from California. They were accommodated in a fenced, stone enclosure complete with large, deep pool, within what is now the gravel garden area of the Plant Nursery. Henry did two feedings at set times on the two afternoons that the garden was open to the public. Sadly, within four years, they became unwell. With Henry and Haroldine away, Dennis Patrick obtained help from Twycross Zoo. The sea lions were diagnosed with a virus from which they did not recover.

Henry replaced the sea lions with two penguins. Children loved to watch them being fed. Monkeys were also temporarily accommodated. During the mid-1970s, however, the decision was taken that apart from the various birds, the keeping of animals for public interest was not worth the huge effort and financial outlay.

Other commercial activities rolled out at Coton Manor. The stable block was converted into a tea room and gift shop, both reached from the stable yard area where the plants were sold (as

they are today). A hexagonal aviary containing budgerigars was positioned around the old black walnut tree to add interest for the visitors.

The garden opened from two until six o'clock on Thursdays, Sundays and Bank Holidays from 1st April to 31st October. The garden was also open on Wednesdays in July and August, whilst during October, the garden could only be visited on Sundays. Opening the garden became a huge commitment from the very beginning.

Visitors taking tea in the stable yard, late-1970s.

Henry was the one to welcome visitors at the gate whilst taking the entry fees. Coton had four macaws at this time, including Emma and Fred. Emma would often be perched on the entrance gate uttering her 'ello' and 'orrible bird' sayings, much to the amusement of the visitors. Haroldine was the plants person, and even on open days could be found tending the garden. Move the clock forward to 1991, and these exact roles would be taken on by their son and his wife, Ian and Susie. Emma's place is now taken by Rodney (of very similar colours), albeit confined to a perch within the stable yard area. Today, it's the family dogs, Alfie and Marmaduke, who provide – very sleepily – the pet interest at the entrance.

Fred and Emma – "Who goes there?" –
1970s.

Alfie and little Marmaduke, 2013.

Coton became known for its unusual perennials. Haroldine became friends with Lady Scott (Valerie Finnis) of Boughton House, who for 28 years was associated with Waterperry Horticultural School for Women, at Waterperry House, situated just outside Oxford. Valerie first went to Waterperry in 1942, aged 18, and helped to make it a famous horticultural institution. She was awarded the Victoria Medal of Honour in 1975 by the Royal Horticultural Society. Haroldine bought many plants from Lady Scott, who with her husband, Sir David Scott, established a very successful alpine nursery. Haroldine and Valerie enjoyed a relationship based on a mutual love of gardening and an exchange of horticultural expertise. It made commercial sense that Coton's plants should be propagated for sale. In the early- to mid-1970s Haroldine did much of this propagating herself. Although the plants were arranged for sale in the stable yard area, as they are today, they were nowhere near the current number.

Yvonne Daw came to work at Coton in 1978 as Head Gardener and worked alongside Haroldine in the garden. Yvonne had trained in horticulture at Moulton College and brought considerable skills in plant propagation. It is from Yvonne's appointment that the selling of plants propagated at Coton became a significant activity. At this time the potting shed was not the brick building we now see by the Herb Garden but the wooden structure to the left of the back of the gift shop. Yvonne and Haroldine had a close-working and mutually respectful relationship. Both had a strong work ethic. It was with great regret that Yvonne said goodbye to Haroldine when she was head-hunted by the owners of Cottesbrooke Hall, Northampton-shire. Yvonne's husband already worked at Cottesbrooke and she was eager to face the challenge of being responsible for the gardens of a much larger establishment. Now retired, Yvonne looks back on her time at Coton Manor as one filled with high activity, and in particular, with fond memories of Haroldine. She also recalls with some pride that she was one of the very few people who could handle Emma the macaw without being bitten!

The opening of the garden from 1969 was only made possible by considerable help from a team of gardeners and other workers. Local ladies did the teas and a Mrs. Roberts came from Ravensthorpe to sell the plants in the old stable yard. George Guerney continued to work at Coton through the 1970s, more as a handyman than a gardener; he worked mainly with Henry building cages for the birds, of which there were many. Dennis Patrick took orders directly from Henry, the Commander, and was mainly concerned with garden construction work. However, Dennis had other talents: he toured the country doing floral arrangement demon-strations. These skills led him to providing flowers for the Spencer family, including Princess Diana, the Queen Mother, and the Pasley-Tyler family weddings. In 1978, and after 25 years of service at Coton, Dennis retired to focus on his floral interests. However, he lives locally, and is full of admiration for how the garden is now maintained, and Susie's skill with plant colours and textures.

In 1979, Richard Green joined the team. He had left school, worked at a printing firm for a few months, and then came to Coton with the intention of staying for just six months in order to gain experience of working with birds. At this time he wished to train as a game keeper and this experience was a necessary condition for course enrolment. However, as often seems to happen at Coton, he came and stayed longer than he initially intended. Within seven years, Henry was saying of Richard: 'He is a hardworking and conscientious person who has also become a very knowledgeable gardener'. He became (and remains) Coton's Head Gardener; his work at Coton stretches across four decades and is significant on several levels as seen in the following chapter. In 1986, Richard was joined by Michael Simon as his assistant. Although Michael was intending to apply for a forestry course starting in the autumn of the year he joined the Coton team, Henry offered him a full-time position after six weeks' work. He accepted and fulfilled what Henry expected of all Coton's workers - to be a 'Jack of all trades'. Henry, Richard and Michael worked on general garden maintenance, construction activities and the care of the birds. Haroldine and Yvonne were more specialist plants people and they maintained the borders. In 1993, Michael left Coton to travel the globe but was drawn back time and time again to work at Coton in the coming decades.

Henry could be a hard task master – but fair and appreciative of peoples' work in the garden. At the end of each day he would assemble the gardeners and say 'Goodbye and thank you for everything you've done today'. He was a hands-on type of person and when moles invaded Goose Park, out he went with a fork during incredibly frosty weather to do battle with the intruders. He lost the battle but eventually won the war. Henry and Haroldine could also be very caring of their staff. Gina Sabbatini, an Italian historian, moved to England with her husband and started working as a cook in the Pasley-Tyler's household in the 1950s. She stayed for several decades, was widowed and then with failing eyesight, decided to retire and return to northern Italy. She was then caught up in the terrible earthquake affecting this region. Hearing of her plight, Henry and Haroldine went to Italy and brought her back to Coton where she stayed and was supported by them as her eyesight continued to decline. Gina died in the early 1990s and is buried at Ravensthorpe.

The first article about Coton Manor garden to appear in *Country Life* was published in July 1987, some 18 years after it opened to the public. One year later, Henry and Haroldine celebrated their 50th wedding anniversary. As part of their celebrations the couple set aside Sunday 15th May for a charity Garden Party; proceeds went to the Peterborough Cathedral Restoration Appeal Fund. The Lord Lieutenant of Northamptonshire, Captain John Lowther CBE, attended and unveiled a new garden seat. He also planted a Ginko tree which still flourishes near the pond, its buttery yellow leaves gloriously complimented by its almost black bark in autumn.

1988: Henry and Haroldine celebrate their 50th wedding anniversary.

Suddenly, and unexpectedly, Haroldine suffered a stroke at Coton Manor on 5th May 1990. She was taken to the intensive care unit at Northampton General Hospital, where she died in the early hours of the following day in the arms of Henry. The funeral was held at St. Denys Church, Ravensthorpe, where almost 52 years previously, she and Henry had married. Coton's garden had been but one part of Haroldine's interest in nature of all kinds and her love of art spanned pictures, opera and music. Well-travelled, outgoing, and entrepreneurial, she was a remarkable woman and exceptionally good company. On the 11th May 1990, St. Denys Church overflowed with those who sought to pay their respects.

Henry was 78 and continued to live on his own at Coton Manor for a few months. On Haroldine's death, their son, Ian, inherited the house but was living with his wife, Susie, in London where they both worked. However, Ian and Susie owned a cottage in Coton. All three decided that the best course of action was for them to swap where they lived in Coton. In January 1991, Henry moved into the cottage that Ian and Susie had purchased in 1987 for their occasional occupation, and they in turn moved into Coton Manor as their main family base. Ian stayed in London during the week for his work, an arrangement that resonates with that of Henry and Haroldine when they first moved into the Manor in 1950. Henry continued to come to the Manor to help with the weekly mowing of the grass. The same gardeners who worked for Henry and Haroldine continued to work for Susie and Ian. Eventually, Henry decided to move to Aynho Park, which at the time consisted of apartments with a residential warden. He still returned to Coton Manor on mowing days whenever he could – just to make sure things were as he thought they should be. He died in December 1995 and is buried with Haroldine at Ravensthorpe.

When next you rest on the bench in the holly bush alcove to admire the wisteria in late spring or the view towards the Loggia, take a look behind you. The seat pays tribute to forty years of hard work – and the great love that Henry and Haroldine shared for their garden.

Haroldine and Henry, the Commander: a tribute.

Susie and Ian Pasley-Tyler

When not at school, Ian Pasley-Tyler recalls a childhood spent largely working outside with his father at Coton Manor, building ponds and canals in the garden. He admits to avoiding being called upon to do horticultural things with his mother, Haroldine, although he could not side-step helping with the weekly processing of poultry from the hen house. On completion of his education, Ian moved to London but regularly returned to Coton Manor at the weekends. He met Susie Methven in 1964 and they were married in the Crypt Chapel at St. Paul's Cathedral in London on 13 December 1967.

Initially, the young couple lived in Albert Street, Camden Town, at a house which had a tiny roof terrace and no garden. Ian and Susie's daughter, Alexandra, was born in July 1971; she was joined by Guy in November 1973. That same year the family moved to another house three doors away. This house had a garden measuring 60ft by 17ft, which like the house, had fallen into neglect and required renovation. Although when they visited Ian's parents at weekends and holidays they often assisted with the garden opening, they did not get involved with the gardening. Their knowledge of gardening was minimal at this time and confined to the demands of managing their small London garden.

Alexandra and Guy were joined by a sister, Imogen, in September 1980. By now Susie was working part-time for an architect. She combined this work and family care with studying for a degree in humanities. By this time Ian's parents, Haroldine and the Commander, were in their mid-seventies. Ian and Susie bought a cottage in the hamlet of Coton in 1987, Imogen was enrolled in a school in the locality, and they spent progressively more time at their Coton home. Ian worked in London during the week and came home for the weekends.

Ian took over the ownership of the Manor in January 1991, several months after Haroldine's unexpected death. Exchanging homes at Coton seemed an ideal arrangement for son and widowed father. It enabled Ian and Susie and their three children to enjoy the space of the Manor and its garden and the Commander found the cottage more appropriate for living on his own. Ian and Susie substantially altered the Manor's kitchen but retained the American refrigerator which had been imported in the 1920s by Ian's grandparents, Harold and Elizabeth. This refrigerator is still functioning! With Ian away in London during the week, Susie worked with the Commander to administer and maintain the Manor's garden for the first two seasons after Haroldine's death. At this time, Ian's sister, Henrietta, and her husband, Nicholas, used the old part of the Manor at weekends. Since Haroldine passed on much of her knowledge of the rare plants in the garden to her daughter, Henrietta's presence at weekends was a valuable source of information. It must have been a difficult time for Susie but she decided to put herself on a steep learning curve to increase her knowledge of plants. She visited many nurseries, read widely, and made visits to locations famous for their plant collections. Any reticence about taking on Coton's garden disappeared as Susie began to understand plants and their nurture.

Ian, Susie and Imogen in Coton's garden: Coton Manor Guide, 1993.

Ian and Susie inherited Coton's two gardeners, Richard Green and Michael (Mike) Simon. Both had largely worked with the Commander on garden maintenance and construction, although they had also assisted with some plant propagation work and planting. Looking after the borders and plant propagation had mainly been Haroldine's and her helpers' responsibility. This situation changed two years after Haroldine's death. First, Ian retired; he no longer needed to commute to London and could give more time to the administration of the estate. That same year, Michael Simon left to fulfil his ambition to travel and explore the world (although he would repeatedly return to work at Coton) and shortly afterwards, John Kimbell began to work in the garden. John lived at Great Brington, near Althorp and came from a family of gardeners; he was exceptionally knowledgeable about plants.

Within three weeks of John starting at Coton, Caroline Tait joined the team as a volunteer. Caroline came with a degree in ecology and within eighteen months of being at Coton, she became a paid - and an increasingly important - member of the team. A division of labour gradually took place. Susie and John became the 'border people', and Caroline became the plant propagator with overall responsibility for the Plant Nursery. Richard was more focused on: hedges, their planting and cutting; lawns, their sowing and mowing; harvesting for and building plant supports and dismantling bird cages; wildfowl, machinery, water courses; developing a number of new garden areas for Susie and John as they progressively focused on improving the aesthetics of the garden.

John Kimbell deserves a special mention as on their own admission, he seems to have had a significant impact on both Susie's and Caroline's horticultural development. Susie was still on her steep learning curve about plants when John joined Coton. John really understood how best to grow plants: the importance of the soil's condition, the choice of location to enable all to flourish, and the grouping of plants to produce an aesthetically pleasing effect. It was he who advised Susie to renovate the borders at Coton and to start from the basic principle of improving the condition of the soil. Taking the borders apart was a bold and brave step, but one which proved to be of enormous benefit to the garden. So John and Susie worked together from 1993 doing just that, stripping the borders, digging in huge quantities of leaf mould, manure and bonfire ash, and then replanting with healthy plants made from splitting existing clumps and new stock. This process took at least six years of collaborative activity. As Susie said at the time: 'We [John and Susie] come at it from different angles. He has a wonderful eye for the shapes of plants and the way they are grouped, while I concentrate on working with colour'. Ian said: 'Getting John was a landmark event. Susie and he are a two-person debating society and one doesn't do anything unless the other is there'. By the end of this process Susie had become a knowledgeable plantswoman and had developed a passion for gardening, which remains undimmed to this day. Also, she had established her preferred way of working in the garden which has stood the test of time, namely alongside someone she can interact with as a sounding board for her ideas.

During this period, Ian and Susie took the decision to scale down the bird population and retain just some of the free range wildfowl. By removing most of the bird shelters and the protective fencing around trees and plants, the garden regained its focus on being a garden rather than a wildlife park. The bird cages had interfered with the vistas throughout the garden, and being chased by aggressive geese was not a pleasant experience. This change in emphasis was also prompted by a visit from Ian's cousin, Anthony du Gard Pasley, a landscape designer and lecturer at the English Gardening School (he could also be easily mistaken for Hercule Poirot!). He complained about the amount of wire everywhere, which he referred to as 'the wirescape'. The taking down of all the bird cages and the removal of the wire fencing was a massive task. As the birds, posts and wire were gradually removed, so the garden took on a whole new ambience.

One of the first changes to signify a greater focus on the aesthetics of the garden occurred in 1993. Susie and Ian had been given roses for their 25th wedding anniversary at the end of

The team at Coton, late-1990s.
(Clockwise: Richard Green, Susie, Ian, Lorenza (Lori) Chapman, John Kimbell, Sue Hill, Caroline Tait).

1992 with the idea that they could be grown to form a Rose Walk. [A Plan of the garden with its named borders is in the Plant List at the end of this book]. The only flat area where this seemed to be practical was the gap between the large fruit cage, which was still being used as an aviary for exotic birds, and the Sea Lion Pool in the Kitchen Garden. A rectangular iron framework was made to bridge this gap and a combination of *Rosa* 'Madame Alfred Carriere' and *Rosa* 'Desprez a Fleurs Jaunes' was planted interspersed with purple *Clematis* 'Jackmanii Superba' and 'Etoile Violette'. A few years later it was decided to soften the angles by installing arches within the rectangular framework; this was a challenge given the limited available space. Later still, the original rectangular structure was removed, leaving just the arches. The same roses can be seen today, with the addition of several *Rosa* 'Ghislaine de Feligonde'. All these roses are scented and repeat flowering in shades of white tinged with pink or with a hint of pale yellow. The Rose Walk not only brought colour and scent into this area and improved its aesthetics, it signified new owners had arrived to take the garden in a different direction and were already using it to signify landmarks in their own lives.

With a greater emphasis on aesthetics, more help than ever was needed in the garden. Volunteers were taken on to supplement the two full-time and one part-time gardeners. Until

1993 the garden opened the same two afternoons of the week as in Haroldine's and the Commander's time but with an increase in the number of visitors. The conversion of the Groom's Cottage into an area for serving lunch prompted the decision to increase the open days to five, and the hours from 12noon until 5.30pm. Ian and Susie also produced an updated guide to the garden in 1993. Unlike its predecessor of 1984, it did not contain a section dedicated to aviculture, and so reflected the change in focus of the garden. However, the large aviary within the Kitchen Garden still existed as a home for peacocks and yellow golden pheasants, and a new macaw, named Rodney, was acquired to replace Emma and Fred sold by Ian's parents. Rodney still lives at Coton; his main residence is in the Kitchen Garden but he has a *pied-à-terre* in the Stable Yard where he entertains visitors on open days.

Rodney at home in the Kitchen Garden, 2015.

In 1994 it was decided to take down the ramshackle old chicken shed which had formed the southern boundary of the Kitchen Garden. About two thirds of the shed was demolished and Susie and Ian decided to fill the newly available, rectangular space with a decorative herb garden. They invited Richard Green to come up with some designs as he had always had an interest in herbs. He did six drawings, signing himself 'Capability Green' much to everyone's amusement, and the one chosen by Susie and Ian is what you see today. Four central, arrow-head shaped beds were edged with *Teucrium chamaedrys* (wall germander). A sundial was placed in the circular bed carpeted with chamomile at the heart of the design. The outer four beds were edged with *Buxus suffruticosa* and the two beds either side of a seat were filled with *Origanum vulgare*. Two honeysuckles were trained as standards for either side of the seat. Richard then planted herbs grown for cooking, medicinal and strewing purposes in the various beds. A new yew hedge was grown to form the boundary of the Kitchen Garden, matching the one already planted at the top of the Rose Bank. By the end of 1994 the majority of the Kitchen Garden with its long asparagus bed and terraces for growing fruit and vegetables had been torn up, sprayed off and turned into the Plant Nursery we see today. The juxtaposition of the remaining Kitchen Garden's espalier fruit trees and vegetables, adds interest to the Plant Nursery area and prevents the whole appearing overly commercial.

Richard Green, 'Capability Green', Head Gardener at Coton Manor.
(By kind permission of Richard Green.)

SUSIE AND IAN PASLEY-TYLER

Stages in the creation of the Herb Garden, 1994–95.

Herb Garden and Rose Walk, 2014.

Haroldine had grown herbs on the steep bank between the Water Garden and the Rose Bank. However, after taking on the garden at Coton, Susie soon realized that these herbs had a tendency to become untidy by mid-season; gravity sent plants – and soil – down the bank. This area is sheltered and faces south, so when the formal Herb Garden was created in 1994, Susie decided to do away with the herbs on the bank in preference for Mediterranean and sun-loving plants. Everything was removed from the bank, railway sleepers were installed to prevent the slippage of soil, and gravel was incorporated to improve the drainage. Then it was planted with a number of sun-loving shrubs and perennials including cistus, helianthemum, rosemary, lavender, phlomis, acanthus, asphodelus, iris, eryngium, thyme, agapanthus, salvia, sedum, and allium. Consequently, this area became known as the Mediterranean Bank. In 2014 it was extended after cutting back and reducing the rhododendrons which had separated it from the adjacent Acer Bank. New logs were inserted to replace the rotting sleepers, and the whole area planted as one, thereby opening up a view to the Water Garden.

The year, 1994, continued to be a particularly busy one at Coton Manor. The on-going removal of the wire fences, posts and gates installed by the Commander to contain birds and protect plants, prompted a reconsideration of how the land could be used. After reducing the number of geese and birds in Goose Park, Ian and Susie had the original field gates and fence removed from the top of this area. The removal of this fence, which was positioned at what is now the middle of the borders at the top of the Park, was a massive task. It took a long time because it was secured with cement, extended two feet underground and sat between well-established plants. Once the fence had been removed, the soil was improved; huge quantities of compost, leaf mould, manure, bonfire ash and gravel were dug in to enhance the soil's quality and drainage. John Kimbell was involved with improving the soil and carrying out the subsequent planting. The colours of the plants in this border were chosen to echo those on the Rose Bank above, namely from a palette of pink, blue, lilac, purple, dark red and white. It has taken many years to get this huge border, known as the Midsummer Border, to look the way it does today.

Old Midsummer Border with wire fence still in situ, 1991.

Midsummer Border, 2014.

Changes in the field beyond Goose Park also took place in 1994. This field was surplus to requirements as a farmed area and when it was annually ploughed in August, Susie and Ian felt that its expanse of brown earth jarred with the green surroundings. They decided to convert it into a Wildflower Meadow; such features were becoming popular at this time. The field was sown with a mixture of grasses and wild flowers in July 1994. Initially, the grasses grew too strongly and obscured any view of the wildflowers. A visitor suggested sowing some yellow rattle, a parasitic annual which reduces the growth rate of grass. The plant was introduced into part of the meadow and encouraged to spread through the collection and sowing of its seed. After two years this treatment showed signs of success. In subsequent years other varieties of wildflowers were introduced, either by the insertion of plug plants, or by sowing seed collected from areas bordering the meadow, as in the case of Ragged Robin. The balance of flowers has changed since that day – and continues to change – fulfilling its promise of becoming another area of interest for visitors. The paths that are mown through the meadow provide an enchanting walk during the height of its flowering season. This area helps to accommodate an ever increasing number of visitors without diminishing the garden's tranquillity.

In 2006, when the flowers were at their peak, the meadow was used for filming one of the circular idents for BBC One. This shows children dancing in a circle with red poppy flowers in the air and is still used between BBC One programmes. Since that filming, the Wildflower Meadow has acquired a new occupant. In 2010, when Ian turned 70, the family purchased a sculpture of a stag. It was installed in the meadow while he was away on holiday so that on the morning of his birthday, it would catch him unawares. Today, as people enter Goose Park and look towards the Wildflower Meadow, it's not unusual to overhear, 'oh look, there's a deer in the next field' and minutes later '... it's not moving at all'. It's a fine piece of art that surprises everyone with its lifelike qualities; it sits well within the meadow, whatever the season.

Wildflower Meadow: plug plants being inserted.

Wildflower Meadow: *ABOVE*: film crew in action, 2006. *BELOW*: 2014.

Ian's 70th birthday present.

In 1996 a Meadow Border was created at the point where the Goose Park terminates with the Wildflower Meadow. This border was planted with daisies, thistles, yarrow, cranesbills and grasses to reflect the types of plants found in the Wildflower Meadow beyond. The border provides a smooth transition from the one area to the other. It is designed with strong colours – oranges, blues and pinks – to make it visible from the top of the Goose Park. The border is actually an island bed and contains a balance of plants providing vertical (agastache and kniphofia) and flat (achilleas, echinaceas and heleniums) flower heads and contrasting growth habits. The Meadow Border exemplifies how Susie and Ian have taken areas of Coton's land and changed them to increase their beauty, whilst enabling them to meld with what already exists.

The Canal Run Border is at the top of the Goose Park where the original field gate was removed, and just below the brick potting shed. It encompasses the Red Border and the Blue and Yellow Border. This area was subjected to the wire removal and soil improvement treatment in 1995-96 and was slowly planted up. There was a huge *Viburnum tomentosum* here; this died and was replaced with a planting of neutral greens, creams and pale yellows to separate the two more pronounced colour schemes of the Red, and Blue and Yellow Borders lying on either side. The Canal Run Border has taken many years to reach its present state. The blue and yellow segment features thermopsis, salvia, lupin, campanula and nepeta in early summer, followed by achilllea, helenium, hemerocallis, kniphofia and herbaceous clematis to take it into autumn.

The red segment is planted with geum, achillea, crocosmia, lobelia, dahlia, penstemon, potentilla and helenium – mainly in shades of red, pale yellows and greens.

In 1999, after the Canal Run Border was finished, it was noticed that only a few people were prepared to walk along the quite steep slope above it to view the planting. So Richard was asked to create a space where people could sit to enjoy the border and the view beyond. He excavated the slope to create a flat area. The soil at the back of this area was then retained with bricks. Nicholas Hodges, a local garden seat designer, was invited to make a pair of semi-circular benches to sit in this space. It has now become very popular with visitors as a place to sit away from the crowd and, on a sunny day, to enjoy the sensation of leaning against warm bricks. My mother and I used to love sitting here.

The Canal Run area below the old hen house, 1985.

Secluded seating area overlooking the Canal Run Border, 2011.

Susie and Ian's first changes to the orchard dimension of Coton Manor date back to 1994 when two new orchards were created, namely Car Park Orchard and Big Moor Orchard. Visitors will be familiar with the first of these because its apple trees border part of the northern boundary of where cars and coaches may park. In 1993, Charles Gregory, who has since become involved in a number of building projects at Coton, obtained heritage apple scions from Brogdale and root stocks from Worcestershire. He processed these and grew them on for a season at his home in France. The stock was surplus to his own needs and Susie agreed to Charles bringing these over from France for use at Coton. Sixty-one different heritage varieties were planted up near the Car Park and fifteen other varieties at the Big Moor location. Both the dessert and cooking apples included early-, mid- and late-season varieties. Photographs show the creation of the Car Park Orchard from initial grafting, growing on in France, and planting at their Coton location. Each year the apples are either sold at Coton or turned into juice, preserves, and puddings in the Café.

Charles teaches Susie how to graft.
(By kind permission of Charles Gregory.)

Apple trees being grown on in France, 1993.
(By kind permission of Charles Gregory)

Setting out the trees in the Car Park Orchard, 1994.
(By kind permission of Jean Reeder)

Fruition.
(By kind permission of Caroline Tait)

Car Park Orchard   **Plan Area 51**

Genus	Species	Cultivar	CommonName
CASTANEA	sativa		Sweet chestnut
MALUS	domestica	'Adam's Pearmain'	Late Dessert (1)
MALUS	domestica	'Annie Elizabeth'	Late Cooking (4)
MALUS	domestica	'Autumn Pearmain'	Med Dessert (4)
MALUS	domestica	'Beauty of Bath'	Early Dessert (2)
MALUS	domestica	'Blenheim Orange'	Late C/D (3T)
MALUS	domestica	'Bramley's Seedling'	Late Cooking (3)
MALUS	domestica	'Charles Ross'	Med C/D (4 S-P)
MALUS	domestica	'Christmas Pearmain'	Late Dessert
MALUS	domestica	'Claygate Pearmain'	Late Dessert (4)
MALUS	domestica	'Cornish Aromatic'	Late Dessert (4)
MALUS	domestica	'Cornish Gilliflower'	Late Dessert (4)
MALUS	domestica	'Crawley Beauty'	Late C/D (3 S-P)
MALUS	domestica	'Discovery'	Early Dessert (3)
MALUS	domestica	'Edward VII'	Late Cooking (6)
MALUS	domestica	'Egremont Russet'	Med Dessert (2)
MALUS	domestica	'Emneth Early'	Early Cooking (1SP)
MALUS	domestica	'Encore'	Late Cooking (4)
MALUS	domestica	'Gascoyne's Scarlet'	Med Dessert (5)
MALUS	domestica	'George Cave'	Early Dessert (2)
MALUS	domestica	'Golden Noble'	Med Cooking (4)
MALUS	domestica	'Idared'	Late Dessert (2)
MALUS	domestica	'Irish Peach'	Early Dessert (4)
MALUS	domestica	'James Grieve'	Early Dessert (3)
MALUS	domestica	'Jester'	Late Dessert (2)
MALUS	domestica	'Jonagold'	Late Dessert (4)
MALUS	domestica	'Katy'	Early Dessert (3)
MALUS	domestica	'Kidd's Orange Red'	Late Dessert (3)
MALUS	domestica	'King's Acre Pippin'	Late Dessert (4T)
MALUS	domestica	'Laxton's Fortune'	Early Dessert (3)
MALUS	domestica	'Laxton's Superb'	Late Dessert (4)
MALUS	domestica	'Laxton's Superb'	Late Dessert (7)
MALUS	domestica	'Lodi'	Early Cooking (5)
MALUS	domestica	'Lord Lambourne'	Med Dessert (2)
MALUS	domestica	'Margil'	Med Dessert (7)
MALUS	domestica	'Merton Charm'	Early Dessert (2)
MALUS	domestica	'Merton Knave'	Early Dessert (3)
MALUS	domestica	'Miller's Seedling'	Early Dessert (3)
MALUS	domestica	'Newton Wonder'	Late Cooking (3SP)
MALUS	domestica	'Nonpareil'	Late Dessert (3)
MALUS	domestica	'Norfolk Beauty'	Med Cooking (2)
MALUS	domestica	'Norfolk Royal'	Med Dessert (5)
MALUS	domestica	'Peasgood 's Nonsuch'	Med Cooking (4)
MALUS	domestica	'Pixie'	Late Dessert (4)
MALUS	domestica	'Ribston Pippin'	Late Dessert (7T)
MALUS	domestica	'Rosemary Russet'	Late Dessert (3)
MALUS	domestica	'Spartan'	Late Dessert (3)
MALUS	domestica	'Sturmer Pippin'	Late Dessert (2)
MALUS	domestica	'Suntan'	Late Dessert (7T)
MALUS	domestica	'Wagener'	Late Dessert (3)

Some of the heritage apple trees in the Car Park Orchard.

Early one morning in June 1996, a loud crash caused Susie and Ian to look out of their bedroom window to see that the huge Japanese pink cherry tree had collapsed into the water. It had overhung the pond and part of the lawn terrace and had been a landmark at Coton for many years. Like the planting of the new orchards, its demise marked the end of one and the beginning of another generation's era at Coton. It was decided to replace the fallen tree with a smaller variety of white cherry, *Prunus* 'Shirotae', deemed by Ian and Susie as more sympathetic in colour and less dominant than its predecessor. A new semi-circular seat to go underneath the new cherry tree was commissioned from Nicholas Hodges. It replaced the white painted seat placed in this area by the Commander in the 1960s. Indeed, since Ian and Susie took over the garden, most of the white seats have been replaced with either teak or iroko versions. This is because they are easier to maintain, and for the most part, appear to blend more easily with the garden. The number of seats has increased hugely throughout the garden in recent years.

Prunus 'Shirotae', planted in 1996.

In 1995 Caroline Tait gained sponsorship from the Merlin Trust to tour commercial nurseries in Ireland and study their propagation methods. The knowledge and skills she gained from this period proved useful at Coton. When Caroline joined Coton in 1993 about 600 plants per year were being propagated and sold with labels made from old yoghurt pots. Today, the most popular plants at Coton are each propagated in numbers of about 300 and the Nursery is responsible for the production of some 45,000 plants, of up to 500 varieties in total. Each year Caroline also presents a popular series of plant propagation events as part of Coton Manor's Garden School programme. She now works three days a week at Coton; the rest of the week she devotes to her own garden design and landscaping business. She continues to lead a committed team of nursery workers at Coton, who between them have gained an excellent reputation for the quality and range of plants they produce. Certainly, the many plants that I've purchased across the years from Coton have done well in my garden. I think this is due to Coton's healthy plant stock and the fact they are well cared for and appropriately hardened off before they go on sale.

Caroline Tait producing plants at Coton Manor.
(By kind permission of Caroline Tait.)

The Plant Nursery with greenhouses, 2015.

With increasing pressure for covered space for the horticultural activities at Coton, in 1997 it was decided to replace the old hen house with a new potting shed. The small wooden potting shed behind the shop that was used in Haroldine's time could no longer accommodate the increasing level of propagation work at Coton. Charles Gregory, Caroline's step-father, was key in the building of the brick potting shed. This is the building we see today in the Plant Nursery and the one used for Caroline's hands-on Garden School propagation events.

The floor being laid in the new potting shed, 1997.

At about the same time, the area beyond the Plant Nursery and greenhouses was levelled and a poly-tunnel erected to house the ever increasing number of propagated plants and pots of tender plants requiring shelter over winter. In 2013 the plant storage area was refurbished with better paths and plant labels to make it more customer-friendly. This involved a considerable amount of work. However, the improvements have proved popular with visitors who are now better able to select the plants they require, given that the stable yard selling area cannot hold the considerable quantity and range of plants that Coton is now able to offer.

Refurbished plant storage / selling area, 2015.

Some of the gardeners assisting Caroline in the Plant Nursery were identified by Susie as being potentially useful to her in developing and maintaining the borders. Sue Hill was one of those and worked alongside Susie in the continuing development of the garden from 1998 until 2006, when she left to settle in New Zealand. Sue came when John Kimbell was still in post but he left within the year; arthritis prevented him from continuing to work at what he loved best. Sue and Susie shared a strong work ethic and they got on well together. Neither snow nor rain deterred their efforts, as can be seen in photographs from the late 1990s. Sue made a significant contribution to the development of the garden during her time at Coton and still keeps in touch with Susie.

Gardening at Coton during the winter months:
Susie Pasley-Tyler and Sue Hill refresh the borders in the late-1990s.

Sue Mappledoram also started as a volunteer in the Plant Nursery in 2006. Susie was very impressed by her general gardening knowledge and enthusiasm. After Sue Hill left for New Zealand, Susie persuaded Sue Mappledoram to help her in the garden. Sue works with Susie in the garden two days a week; the rest of the week she is a science teacher. Sue has become Susie's gardening soulmate as well as a good friend. As Susie says: 'We sing from the same hymn sheet when it comes to gardening … and we do indeed sing in a choir together too!'. Two of Caroline's helpers in the Plant Nursery, Sally Humphrey and Liz Reader, also spend a day each helping Susie in the garden. This provides a useful interaction between the garden and the Nursery: it helps the gardeners to know what is required for propagation, whether plants are available in the Nursery, and where they are located.

The Garden School was started in 1994 and was run by a local garden designer. Unfortunately, it gradually ran down during the following years and became unviable. However, in 1997 Ian and Susie took on the running of the School themselves and the programme for 1999 shows their choice of an eclectic mix of speakers covering a range of topics. This was the way forward and the Garden School continues to flourish to this day. Its success is down to good organisation, provided by Coton's Administrator, Sarah Patterson, and a mix of hands-on events as well as excellent speakers. What better location in which to extend one's understanding of gardening? With an informal, friendly atmosphere, and a very good lunch included, it is not surprising that vouchers for these events are often given as presents.

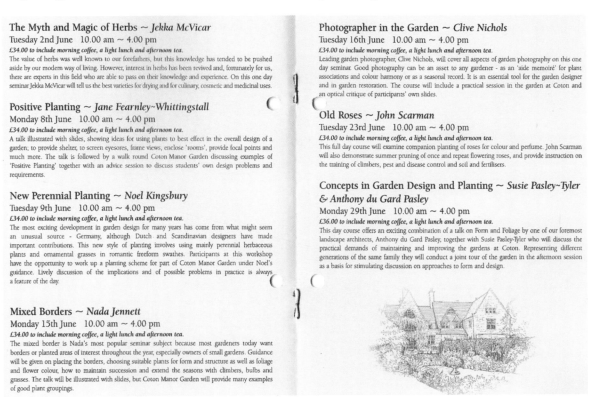

The Myth and Magic of Herbs ~ *Jekka McVicar*
Tuesday 2nd June   10.00 am ~ 4.00 pm
£34.00 to include morning coffee, a light lunch and afternoon tea.
The value of herbs was well known to our forefathers, but this knowledge has tended to be pushed aside by our modern way of living. However, interest in herbs has been revived and, fortunately for us, there are experts in this field who are able to pass on their knowledge and experience. On this one day seminar Jekka McVicar will tell us the best varieties for drying and for culinary, cosmetic and medicinal uses.

Positive Planting ~ *Jane Fearnley-Whittingstall*
Monday 8th June   10.00 am ~ 4.00 pm
£34.00 to include morning coffee, a light lunch and afternoon tea.
A talk illustrated with slides, showing ideas for using plants to best effect in the overall design of a garden; to provide shelter, to screen eyesores, frame views, enclose 'rooms', provide focal points and much more. The talk is followed by a walk round Coton Manor Garden discussing examples of 'Positive Planting' together with an advice session to discuss students' own design problems and requirements.

New Perennial Planting ~ *Noel Kingsbury*
Tuesday 9th June   10.00 am ~ 4.00 pm
£34.00 to include morning coffee, a light lunch and afternoon tea.
The most exciting development in garden design for many years has come from what might seem an unusual source - Germany, although Dutch and Scandinavian designers have made important contributions. This new style of planting involves using mainly perennial herbaceous plants and ornamental grasses in romantic freeform swathes. Participants at this workshop have the opportunity to work up a planting scheme for part of Coton Manor Garden under Noel's guidance. Lively discussion of the implications and of possible problems in practice is always a feature of the day.

Mixed Borders ~ *Nada Jennett*
Monday 15th June   10.00 am ~ 4.00 pm
£34.00 to include morning coffee, a light lunch and afternoon tea.
The mixed border is Nada's most popular seminar subject because most gardeners today want borders or planted areas of interest throughout the year, especially owners of small gardens. Guidance will be given on placing the borders, choosing suitable plants for form and structure as well as foliage and flower colour, how to maintain succession and extend the seasons with climbers, bulbs and grasses. The talk will be illustrated with slides, but Coton Manor Garden will provide many examples of good plant groupings.

Photographer in the Garden ~ *Clive Nichols*
Tuesday 16th June   10.00 am ~ 4.00 pm
£34.00 to include morning coffee, a light lunch and afternoon tea.
Leading garden photographer, Clive Nichols, will cover all aspects of garden photography on this one day seminar. Good photography can be an asset to any gardener - as an 'aide memoire' for plant associations and colour harmony or as a seasonal record. It is an essential tool for the garden designer and in garden restoration. The course will include a practical session in the garden at Coton and an optical critique of participants' own slides.

Old Roses ~ *John Scarman*
Tuesday 23rd June   10.00 am ~ 4.00 pm
£34.00 to include morning coffee, a light lunch and afternoon tea.
This full day course will examine companion planting of roses for colour and perfume. John Scarman will also demonstrate summer pruning of once and repeat flowering roses, and provide instruction on the training of climbers, pest and disease control and soil and fertilisers.

Concepts in Garden Design and Planting ~ *Susie Pasley-Tyler & Anthony du Gard Pasley*
Monday 29th June   10.00 am ~ 4.00 pm
£36.00 to include morning coffee, a light lunch and afternoon tea.
This day course offers an exciting combination of a talk on Form and Foliage by one of our foremost landscape architects, Anthony du Gard Pasley, together with Susie Pasley-Tyler who will discuss the practical demands of maintaining and improving the gardens at Coton. Representing different generations of the same family they will conduct a joint tour of the garden in the afternoon session as a basis for stimulating discussion on approaches to form and design.

1999: Part of the Garden School Programme.

Caroline Tait's propagation class.

One of Richard Green's plant supports in Coton's garden.

Class of 2013 aspiring to Richard's example.

Tom Duncan's talk on Irish Gardens, 2014.

Sarah Patterson welcoming people to a Garden School event, coffee on hand.
(By kind permission of Sarah Patterson.)

It was during the 1990s that the sculpture, 'Pan', was purchased by Ian and Susie from the sculptress, Mary Cox. This figure sits very well in its yew alcove and looks particularly good when surrounded by white tulips in spring. Turn right in front of 'Pan' and one is at the top of the Water Garden; turn left and the lush, green carpet of the Woodland Garden beckons.

The woodland area's boundary fence, which had been installed by the Commander in the 1960s, cut across what had originally been part of the garden. This seemed to be indicated by the crop of snowdrops growing on both sides of the fence. In 2001 Ian and Susie decided to remove this fence and reinstate the boundary further back into part of the nearby field (Big Moor). This allowed the snowdrops to become part of the garden again. Simultaneously, it provided an opportunity to renew and realign the gate into the field and garner

'Pan', by Mary Cox.

a view towards the Reservoir below the garden; a 'tired' beech hedge had hitherto obscured this view. A hedge of native plants was introduced on the inside of the newly positioned fence and the extra space was used to create a path meandering through the woodland. Increasing the size of the Woodland Garden has allowed for three discrete areas to evolve: under the copper beech planted with special spring bulbs, trilliums, erythroniums, epimediums, woodland anemones and leucojums; a large round bed bordered by the path, which is planted with herbaceous woodlanders including hellebores, hardy geraniums,

Part of the Woodland Garden, 1960s.

pulmonarias, ferns, campanulas, aconitums, anemones and tricyrtis; and beyond these two areas, a more naturalized space full of snowdrops, aconites, primroses, bluebells and whitebells.

The same part of the Woodland Garden, 2014.

Returning to 'Pan's' alcove area, it is but a short step to the top of the Water Garden. The whole of the Water Garden requires constant maintenance due to the combined effects of frost and the force of the water from nearby springs. The wetter and colder the winter, the more likely is the need to repair the concrete in this area. In the early 2000s, Ian and Susie replaced the wooden hut at the bottom of the Water Garden. Michael Simon had returned to work at the Manor at this time and he and Richard built a fine, rustic summer house. Below this summer house there was a neglected, wild area consisting of elder and bamboo under a few trees. The stream from the Water Garden had previously been piped underground in this area to service the Lower Orchard. In 2003 the bamboo, elder and the pipe were removed, and with the aid of a digger, Richard changed the contours of the ground. This enabled the previously piped water to form a stream, which in turn created a damp area suitable for bog plants. He built a footbridge across the stream and it was decided to use tall plants with large foliage to create a rather different effect from the Water Garden. Japanese primulas, Siberian iris and zantedeschias were positioned in and beside the water and varieties of rodgersia, persicaria, darmera, astilbe, hemerocallis hostas, ferns, filipendulas and euphorbias were used to clothe the beds beyond the water's edge.

More construction work took up Richard's time and ingenuity as he reinstated the rill in the Old Orchard. The two ponds created by the Commander for the wildfowl were removed and a rill (the same length as the one originally positioned here in the 1920s) was inserted. The new version has a dip in each tread to enhance the cascade effect. The original rill had square pools at its mid-point and both ends; these were not re-established.

Rill in the Old Orchard.

Looking up the original rill,
late-1920s.

Looking down the reinstated rill,
early-2000s.

In the years since the reinstallation of the rill, Susie and Ian have continued to develop a spring meadow in the Old Orchard. Some snowdrops had already been planted here in the early 1990s and in 1998 they were joined by patches of the naturalizing *Crocus tommasinianus* to provide a glorious carpet of white and purple flowers in spring. Seeds of *Primula veris* (cowslip) and bulbs of pheasant's eye narcissus, blue *Camassia leichtleinii, Fritillaria meleagris, Tulipa sylvestris* and *Ornithogalum nutans* have since joined them. Over the years bulbs of *Tulipa* 'Spring Green', lifted from pots after flowering, have been planted individually; these continue to proliferate. Some of the old fruit trees planted in the 1920s have died or collapsed and so in early 2015, six new trees were introduced (two pear, one plum, an apricot, a cherry and a greengage). In spring, with the tinkling of water from the rill, blossom on the trees, and the scent and colours of the naturalized flowers, this is my favourite place to sit and 'just be' for a while.

From the very beginning of taking over the garden, Susie and Ian considered the old Sea Lion Pool as an unsatisfactory area. However, the Pool was a substantial structure and the cost of its complete removal was prohibitive. In 2004 it was finally decided to convert it into a gravel garden. This provided an opportunity to grow plants which need their own space and might otherwise become swamped or overlooked in a border. Now this area contains many varieties of sun-loving plants including, eryngium, erysimum, euphorbia, agapanthus, dierama, iris, helianthemum, species paeonies, pulsatilla, alliums, shrubby potentillas, and eremurus.

Aviary and drained Sea Lion Pool, 1992.

Gravel Garden, 2004.

In 2005, the year before Sue Hill left Coton for New Zealand, major work took place in the Rose Garden near the Loggia. The roses in this area were suffering from rose sickness and despite everyone's best efforts, they continued to decline. All the roses were removed and the soil was replaced. Susie decided not to replant with new roses but rather to change the planting to one requiring minimal watering, feeding and staking. Some evergreens were introduced to provide interest during the winter months. Five years later, once the beds had proved to be disease free, a group of three *Rosa* 'Little White Pet' was introduced to each of the four quadrant beds. The Rubbio-inspired well-head was retained at the centre of the design. To my mind, this always looks best when filled with white flowering plants. Note that in the photographs of this time the yew hedge has been cut back hard to promote new, dense growth.

Rose Garden, 2005: Richard and Michael remove the roses and old soil.

New soil added and levelled.

Susie and Sue Hill replant the quadrant beds.

Haroldine and the Commander had used the greenhouse in the old Kitchen Garden to create a tropical effect. In 2007 Ian and Susie put this space to another use. The interior low stone wall and wall fountain were removed; the floor was levelled and then covered with gravel. Raised benches were built and installed on either side along the entire length of the greenhouse; these changes provided much needed space for the sale of tender plants. The wall fountain, which had been positioned inside at the mid-point, was carefully removed and 'recycled' to sit outside, close to the doorway.

Michael and Richard gutting the greenhouse, 2007.

Temperate House now used to sell tender plants.

Wall fountain repositioned outside the greenhouse.

The keeping of free-range bantams at Coton was inspired by a visit to Rousham, where Ian and Susie had seen a collection of Mille Fleur Barbu D'Uccle birds roaming the courtyard area. Coton now has a flock of about forty of these brightly coloured creatures and they provide endless entertainment for everyone with their constant searching for worms. Two Longhorn cows were acquired in 2007 and these have now produced a small herd which fluctuates between seven and eleven animals; this is really as many as Big Moor (the field beyond the Woodland Garden) can support. This small herd is looked after by Richard and Sally. Young bulls are slaughtered at thirty months and the meat is sold at Coton when available; it is very popular. The orchard at the top of Big Moor is also home to a collection of Kunekune pigs; during the autumn months, they feast on the windfall apples. These delightful animals are kept for the pleasure of their company rather than as a source of food.

Longhorn cows at Coton, 2014.

Kunekune pigs, 2014.

One doesn't have to stay long at Coton before realising that maintenance and refurbishment are on-going. The winter months are the busiest of the year for all those working at Coton. From the end of September Susie and the gardeners work flat out replenishing the borders. Winter pruning and the planting of trees and shrubs also takes place. For example, during the winter of 2011, the old privet hedge at the back of the pond and the top of the Mediterranean Border was taken out by Richard and replaced with yew. Later, the decision was taken to prune the two old yews near the 1662 front door. Hard-pruning is an understatement, but a necessary step for reshaping these trees and stopping them overshadowing the nearby borders and lawn. Both trees have put on new growth, showing how forgiving yews can be when cut back to old wood. An area that was continually damp between the Woodland Garden and the pond was changed from grass to paving in 2013, and with the addition of a seat, now makes a pleasant, dry seating area. It is a particularly pleasant spot to sit in early spring as it affords lovely views of the many varieties of hellbores flowering beneath the mature trees.

During the winter of 2014-15, the entire length of the stone wall supporting the Holly Hedge Terrace was dismantled and then rebuilt from the existing stone. Apart from a few sinks on the terraces, this is the only area of the garden which is suitable for alpine plants. The rebuilding of the wall, which was showing signs of collapsing, has allowed for the removal of perennial weeds which were embedded in the stonework. It has also provided an opportunity to plant the wall in a more coherent and less random fashion, although it is mainly the same cast of plants that were there before. Looking at it now, one would never know it is a new wall; it should retain the terrace for a good number of years to come.

Examples of work conducted in recent years at Coton.

Yiannis (son-in-law of Dennis Patrick) rebuilding the
Holly Hedge Terrace stone wall in 2014.

Yews showing re-growth after Richard's hard pruning in 2013.

The restaurant area, which is now used during inclement weather and for Garden School lunches, was run as a commercial restaurant for a time during the 1990s. It was known as 'Groom's Cottage Restaurant', named after this building being originally occupied by the estate's groom during the 1920s and 1930s. The restaurant was open through the winter months at weekends (Friday and Saturday evenings and Sunday lunchtime). Anne Thompson-Royds was the chef running the restaurant but in 1999 she left to go freelance and the restaurant reverted to being used as additional space for the Café's activities. Throughout the opening season, Coton's Café provides food for many thousands of people. Coach parties are catered for, often several on the same day, two course lunches are provided for Garden School events, and a phenomenal number of sandwiches and slices of cake are sold during the summer months. A largely unseen, surprisingly small team of ladies, mostly drawn from local villages, take credit for this feat of catering. It's all done with style and even on the busiest of days when the kitchen is stretched to the limit, one never feels rushed as a visitor. Lorenza (Lori) Chapman started working in the Plant Nursery and in the Kitchen helping Anne Thompson-Royds. Since Anne left to go freelance, Lori and Janet Reader have been running the Kitchen. Lori's lasagne is legendary – well, she is Italian. Currently unwell, it is hoped she will return soon. Gill Brown has been in charge of the Café and organising staff since about 1995. Several thousands of jars of jams, jellies and chutneys are produced for sale in Coton's kitchen by Sylvia Muddiman. Sylvia started working at Coton as the Housekeeper in October 1996, and she has helped in the Café's kitchen for many years on an ad hoc basis.

Some of the Café staff across time.

Left to right: Alicia, Janet, Alice, Lori, Gill.

Sylvia making jam.

When Susie and Ian inherited the garden in 1991 there were formal beds of roses in the Rose Garden, a number of rugosa roses on the Rose Bank, the wonderful 'Seven Sisters' rose on the south side of the house, and scarlet roses in the Holly Hedge Border. Twenty five years later there are roses everywhere – in borders, up trees, as specimens in the more open areas, on walls, on frames over water, in the orchards – anywhere Susie can accommodate them as they are her favourite flower. There is a humorous point of contention with Head Gardener, Richard Green, who claims not to like roses, and pretends to groan every time he sees another one being planted. This is particularly the case if the new rose is up a wall or tree, which will require him to add it to his pruning activities. It's become a sort of game for Susie and Sue Mappledoram to see whether they can plant another rose without him noticing. The Rose Bank is now home to about forty different types of rose, including some of the original rugosas. About half of these are repeat-flowering forms and they are in a variety of shades of pink and white. The companion planting echoes these colours and also includes blues, purples and some pale yellows.

The roses in the Rose Garden are now mostly on the walls and in the beds surrounding the central quadrant beds. On the whole, the colours of these roses tend towards a more yellow rather than a blue shade of pink and this is reflected in the quadrant and surrounding beds where there are groups of erysimum, diascia, dahlia, dianthus, cleome, penstemon all echoing this shade of pink.

There are many roses growing up trees which have taken a considerable time to establish; there are those in borders, some of which are supported on the hazel and willow frames that Richard is renowned for creating, and others are freestanding. Roses at Coton have not been sprayed for years, but they are kept healthy with large amounts of manure in spring. Repeat-flowering forms are given an application of chicken manure pellets after their first flowering. In dry periods the roses are kept moist with the help of a leaky pipe system. Most of the roses are pruned hard through the winter and early spring and are constantly deadheaded in summer to show them to best advantage.

One of the many features that strike visitors to Coton is the number of pots decorating the house terraces and other parts of the garden. Susie inherited an interesting collection of pelargoniums and tender perennials from her mother-in-law, Haroldine, and this collection has expanded over the years. This is in part due to Caroline Tait's acquisition of more interesting plant specimens from her visits to flower shows, and from sourcing specialist suppliers. The pots are mostly planted up with a single variety and then placed as: singles; pairs where there is a formal space; in groups of similar and complementary colours. Susie considers that this makes it easier to remove a pot when the contents have gone over. There are also a few pots with mixed plantings but it is the collection of scented leaf pelargoniums, many inherited from Haroldine, which is probably the strongest component of many of the pots. Whenever possible, these are placed beside seats and on low walls where they can be touched and the different scents appreciated by visitors. The subject of planting up pots is a regular – and oversubscribed – feature on the Garden School programme.

Rose Bank, 1991.

Rose Bank, 2014.

Rose Garden wall with fuschia, hemerocallis and lavender, 1991.

Rose Garden wall with *Rosa* 'Gardener's Pink', 2014.

Pots on the Loggia's terrace, 2014.

From the time they took over Coton in 1991, Ian dealt with visitors, plant sales, and had oversight of the organisation of the Café and Garden School, while Susie was responsible for the garden. This arrangement has held to the present day. Besides being responsible for the Vegetable Garden and working in the Nursery, Michelle Bales helps Ian regularly on the admission gate on Saturdays; during the week he is assisted by several local ladies. Sarah Patterson works closely with Ian on the estate's administration and it is normally her voice that one hears when telephoning Coton Manor to enquire about visiting the garden or attending a Garden School event. Sarah has been working at Coton for some twenty years; her work is multifaceted and at busy times, requires a capacity to multi-task as well as a calm head.

When Susie is asked how she feels the garden has changed during the years that she and Ian have been living at Coton, she says they have introduced variety to the ambience of the garden by taking advantage of Coton's different aspects and types of soil, and by using different types of planting. Ian's answer to this question is that the planting throughout the garden has changed enormously since his parents' time, largely due to Susie's influence. My answer is that the garden has cleverly changed from being inward looking to capturing and composing balanced views of the surrounding countryside without losing its sense of intimacy; harmony now reigns. People who have known the garden across the generations say that the standard of maintenance is now exceptional and that 'it has just got better and better'.

A composed view: harmony achieved between the Goose Park and the
Wildflower Meadow beyond, 2014.

Coton Manor garden has drawn many plaudits since Ian and Susie took it over in January 1991. These include articles in *Country Life* and gardening magazines, Susie's series of seasonal accounts of gardening at Coton in *Hortus*, and appearing in the television programmes, Chris Beardshaw's *Flying Gardener* and *Gardener's World*. They all testify to the high regard with which Coton Manor's designed landscape is held. The *Daily Telegraph's* competition, in which the public were invited to nominate their favourite garden, saw Coton Manor securing third position, ahead of several large gardens in the care of national bodies, and the only private garden amongst the top three. The achievements since 1991 are clearly the result of a huge team effort but the aesthetic improvements within the garden are mainly due to Susie Pasley-Tyler's guiding hand, which has become increasingly more skilful across the years. One only has to talk to Susie for a short time to know that the garden is her passion. Her attention to detail for achieving accord in colour, texture and plant association is quite extraordinary. She 'sees' the garden as an artist would, and composes horticulturally perfect 'pictures' throughout the seasons, yet on her own admission, has neither drawing nor painting skills.

As an academic I've researched the history of many gardens, and particularly those dating back to Tudor and Stuart times, for which, generally, there are no surviving accounts of why and how the gardens were made. I have often wished that I could speak with the creators of these spaces to access their thinking and the nature of their experiences as they gardened. So I asked Susie to talk to me about her passion for Coton's garden and obtained her permission to record what was said in the following chapter. Perhaps in time to come, a future garden historian will thank me!

Susie Pasley-Tyler:
a personal reflection
'Gardening to make you smile'

It was a rather cold, November day in 2013 when I first spoke to Susie about her involvement in Coton's garden. I wouldn't call it an interview, rather more of an informal chat and it was over a mug of tea in Coton's warm kitchen, but it did what I wanted it to. This was to reveal what the garden means to her and the extent to which she is hands-on in its creation and maintenance. The year had been the wettest on record and spring had come late. I asked Susie how this had affected Coton's garden.

"The weather has allowed everything to develop slowly. All the shrubs have performed well but particularly the roses, yes, the roses were fantastic and we've had a wonderful crop of fruit with loads of apples. There have been one or two exceptions: the pears weren't so good and nor were the greengages, but we have got a monumental crop of apples and damsons, quinces and plums."

"What have you done with it all?"

"A lot of it has already been converted into jam for sale in the Café and Shop: gooseberry and elderflower, apple and pear, plum, damson and quince cheese – Sylvia, our housekeeper, has been working flat out. I'd have to check this, but I think she's talking about 3,000 jars of jams, jellies, marmalades, chutney and quince cheese."

"Fruit apart, you say the shrubs have done well?"

"Yes, the shrubs have grown phenomenally well. We weren't so conscious of it during the summer, but when we started to go through the borders in October after the garden closed, we suddenly realized that some groups of plants were swamping others. So, we've been pruning and giving everything its own space rather than allowing one plant to merge into the next one – terribly important as otherwise you lose the individual shapes of things. But I can never remember another season in the 23 years we have gardened here when there has been so much growth … I think it's largely due to the wet, plus eventually we did get some sun and warmth which must have helped as well."

The Old Orchard.

"Do you use particular months for reviewing the garden – what's to be chopped, what's to be taken out, what's to be altered?"

"To some extent it happens continuously throughout the year but we always examine the borders during August and September while things are still visible. We decide what's got too big and what we would like to replace. We might put in something new where colours are not absolutely right. Quite often I walk round with a flower or twig in my hand to see where it would look best because if you don't do it then, you can't possibly remember the exact colour in the winter. We make notes on all parts of the garden in those two months."

"Do you make the notes or does one of the gardeners do it?"

"I make them in concert with Sue [Mappledoram] and then we compare them in case one of us cannot decipher the inevitable shorthand!"

In all of Susie's comments the 'we' refers to herself and Coton's team of gardeners, but in recent years to Sue Mappledorham in particular. Susie enters the handwritten notes that she makes as she goes around the garden onto her laptop to form a running commentary about the state of the garden. Already in our chat it is clear that Susie is continuously monitoring the garden's horticultural state and is definitely hands-on. The team of gardeners are mostly part-time, fitting in Coton work with family, study and other work commitments; some are volunteers.

"As soon as the garden is closed in early October we start work on the Woodland Garden. This is the first part of the garden to start flowering in late winter and early spring. So any

BERBERIS BED

Remove G. Patricia
Remove Sanguisorba obtusa
Remove Aster divaricatus
Remove Rodgersia Chocolate Wings
Remove Lythrum Robert
Remove Tradescantia
Remove Centaurea
Plant another group of Bidens to left of Persicaria Red Dragon
Plant Agastache Blue Fortune in front of bidens
Lift and plant Crocosmia solfaterre behind Geum
Run Geranium Blue Cloud behind and left of Euphorbia pasteurii
Campanula lactiflora Prichard's Var. to go between Kniphofia Percy's Pride and Crocosmia solfaterre
Crocosmia solfaterre to go to right of Campanula
Caryopteris Dark Knight x 3 to go in front of Crocosmia
Move some Kniphofia Wrexham Buttercup back where Lythrum Robert has come out
Bring Geranium magnificum forward to front and left of Potentilla
Find space near Euphorbia pasteurii for another group of Kniphofia Percy's Pride
Increase Echinacea White Swan & bring forward to bridge gap at front between iris and Kniphofia Wrexham Buttercup
Plant Rosa Autumn Sunset x 3 (when available) to left of Geranium magnificum
Plant Nepeta subsessilis in front of Artemisia lact. Ghuizo, behind Aster Wunder von Staffe
Plant Potentilla recta Sulphureum behind Rosa alba semiplena
Plant Thermopsis lanceolata to left of Geranium magnificum and behind Rosa Autumn Sunset
Move several plants of Aster Wunder von Staffe left into space vacated by Sanguisorba obtuse
Plant Dahlia ?orange cactus x 3 behind Iris Sable

BLUE & YELLOW BORDER

Reverse Clematis Cassandra and Thermopsis
Switch Echinacea Sunrise (find more if poss) with shrubby Potentilla
Lift yellow herbaceous Potentilla sulphureum and plant in place of Geranium Patricia, which has to come out
Lift and plant Iris Dusky Skies where Potentilla sulphureum has come out
Move group of Verbena away from Agastache to go behind Dahlia Helen
Lift Verbena between Helenium, Baptisia & Helianthus and add to group to left of Galega, making more space to left of current verbena planting by shifting righthand side of Aconitum Kelmscott to left to disguise Lupins and Thalictrum
Find another blue for vacated Verbena space - Salvia amistad
Bring Lysimachia forward to abut Helianthus (reducing Helianthus)
Leave Hemerocallis dumorteri next to Lysimachia
Leave both Lupin Chandelier and Campanula lactiflora where there is space after other moves
Move some Achillea Anthea from right to left spot vacated by Crocosmia
Move Galega behind Hemerocallis dumorteri
Plant Clematis Cassandra behind Achillea Anthea & in front of Hemerocallis
Leave both Lupin Chandelier and Campanula lactiflora where there is space after other moves

Pages from Susie's 2014 garden notebook.

work here needs doing before the massive amount of leaves from the tree canopy fall and obscure what is underneath. If we start work here in early October, it also allows any plants that have been dug up or newly planted to recover in time for the following year. Then as it's still too early to plant tulips [a task for November and December] we look at our notes and tackle any of the more major changes that we've planned. While plants are still standing it enables you to see the space they are going to need and their heights and, to some extent, colours. Once everything has either died or been cut down, it's easy to lose one's sense of what is where. I know roughly where things are but you often need to go and read a label to remind yourself and then you have to think 'Ah, six foot or two foot; blue or white etc.' Doing major changes in October does help to avoid overplanting."

"What happens from November?"

"From November we start going through all the borders, commencing with the ones where tulips will be planted. This involves cutting back, inevitable leaf clearance, weeding, reducing some groups while increasing others, lifting plants for propagation, adding new plants, pruning roses and any shrubs that haven't been summer-pruned … planting tulips and perhaps other bulbs, checking and writing labels - and, finally, mulching with our own compost."

"So what are you changing during the months of October 2013 to March 2014?"

"Earlier this year we did a lot in the Water Garden, partly because we had a terrible leak. We've got springs at Coton and we are never quite sure whether it's an existing water channel [a designed feature] – most of which are cemented and can crack in cold weather – or whether it's a spring that is coming up. The area in the lower part of the Water Garden was completely water-logged early in the spring and I had to take out a lot of the white anemone 'Honorine Jobert' and one or two other thing including, sadly, *Cercis canadensis* 'Forest Pansy', the Judas tree with the beautiful dark red foliage. It died because it was too wet there. So then I put in *Rodgersia aesculifolia*, monarda, trollius and siberian iris - plants that could cope with the wet conditions."

"That's a substantial bit of new planting."

"Yes, it was, and since we closed I've been back to work there because that was all done in a bit of a panic in April. I hope I have made sense of the rest of it now. That was a major job and then I did a whole lot of work in the Mid-summer Border because I decided that I had too many spires [plants that produce tall spikes of flowers]. It's a border which is at its best from July to September but there are a lot of plants which have these slender spires [aconitums, veronicas, verbascums, lythrums and cimicifugas]. Some are needed, but you don't want to overdo it. This year the clumps seem to have got bigger, some had merged together and the vertical effect was so much more pronounced. So I have had to reduce some of the groups and I've separated what's left by inserting plants with a different growth habit. I spent ages rearranging them but it is certainly easier to do it while the surrounding planting is standing and colours are still apparent."

"So is it a case of digging up the whole clump of a flowering plant?"

"Sometimes we do, it depends what it is and whether we want to move the whole group, which we did in one or two instances, and of course whether we need material for propagation.

The Mid-summer Border. *ABOVE:* Before changes. *BELOW:* After changes.

There was also an aster which prompted some of the alterations. It's called 'Harrington's Pink', a lovely clear pink, unusually so. You know how quite a lot of asters are a sort of indeterminate bluish-mauve … you can't really put your finger on it. But this is a good, fresh pink, yet every so often some of the mauve flowers would emerge in the middle of the group. I thought we must have got it confused with another variety, but I finally decided it was some form of reversion – so out it came, creating another space!"

"But you lost your lovely pink?"

"Yes, but I've got other pinks and since everything was late this year, most of the asters didn't flower until after we closed. So it was a good moment to reduce their numbers. I have mixed feelings about asters. Apart from flowering rather late for when the garden is open to the public, many need supporting and aside from forms of *A.* x *frikartii*, and unusual ones like *A. divaricatus*, they are not amongst my favourite flowers. The garden can become rather over-'daisified' in September, if one is not careful."

"So you don't alter the garden's structure a great deal? You're normally only altering the planting each year? Is that because you've got to the point where the structure is permanent?"

"Yes, I think we have more or less reached that point. We do minor things … there was an unfortunate bit of crazy-paving by the front door. We have changed that this winter. We have also taken a large acacia tree out of one of the bigger borders. It had the rose 'Alister Stella Gray' growing up it. It looked glorious for a month, but after that, it looked a mess. We couldn't deadhead the rose – way out of our reach – and the tree itself was gradually dying. Also it was difficult to plant round the base of the tree as the ground was full of roots and impossibly dry. It's much better out and has given me the opportunity to spread the plants out … so everything now has more space. There were originally four of these acacia trees in this area - all gone now. But we still call it The Acacia Border."

These words about Susie's recent activities in the garden appear to resonate with her general beliefs about gardening.

"I think one of the things I have gradually learnt in life generally, is the truth of the maxim, 'Less is More'. This is particularly true of gardening and it has become a guiding principle for me. It's tempting to put a plant in an available space, especially when the garden is young and one wants to cover the soil. My approach is to use a limited palette of plants in a border and a fair amount of repetition. By repetition I mean using different varieties of the same plant – and repeating shapes and the colours of flowers and foliage. Of course, I also include single and specimen plants for emphasis in the borders, and there are plants that are not repeated … repetition is particularly suited to the bigger borders, and it does seem to be pleasing to the eye."

Susie then reveals how she controls the repetition of plants and colour to achieve harmony in the garden. Colour is clearly one of her primary concerns.

"I have in my mind a rough colour theme and a limited selection of plants for each border. So when you go round the garden each border should create a different impression without too much repetition from one place to another. Of course there are some plants which appear in several different parts of the garden – such as, *Campanula lactiflora* and agastache in sunnier parts and hellebores and ferns in shadier areas. These are the ones that spring to mind, but there

The Acacia Border.
ABOVE: The last remaining tree. *BELOW:* Tree removed giving more space and light.

are many more. In this garden we are fortunate to enjoy quite a range of aspects and soil conditions. These range from dry shade in the Woodland Garden to partial and damp shade in the Water and Bog Gardens, and to full sun in the more exposed areas of the garden. The top parts of the garden are fairly sheltered, whilst the lower parts are more exposed to winds and frost. Most of the garden is on clay but the soil in the lower areas has a sandier texture. So we can grow a wide range of plants, and this increases the opportunities to create different moods and effects."

"Could you show me how this works in a particular border? Can you give me an example?"

"Yes, for example if you look at the photograph of the Acacia Border it might give you some idea of what I am trying to achieve. When we took the garden over there were a number of self-set purple honesty [*Lunaria annua*] and sweet rocket [*hesperis*] in this border and a lot of large-leaf, early-performing plants with good foliage – cardoons, euphorbias, tree paeonies and echinops. I realized that this was the first border to look good at the time we open the garden in spring. That prompted me to think that I should aim for a 'best moment' in each border, hopefully peaking at different times. Then the mauves and purples of the honesty and rocket persuaded me to pursue this colour scheme throughout the year for this border. There are also blues, whites, pale pinks and some dark reds, and in the spring, a little yellow - but pink/purple is dominant."

Susie explains how she uses different plants for each season in a particular border to keep the same colour palette going throughout the year. She starts by emphasizing that for each season she uses the same plant in several places in the border. It's all about achieving a harmonious whole.

"So, initially we use about six or seven groups of a tulip called 'Negrita' which is exactly the same colour as the Honesty. Just overlapping in time and echoing the tulip colour are five or six groups of *Allium* 'Purple Sensation'. Then come the dark reds of *Astrantia* 'Claret' – three groups of these - and *Paeonia delavayii*, and several groups of pale pink aquilegias and *Thalictrum aquilegifolium* - and the pink cow parsley, *Chaerophyllum hirsutum* 'Roseum'. Taking out the last remaining acacia tree has allowed me to place some of these early performers nearer the back of the border. They will all need cutting back – some to reflower and others just to re-leaf. The next stage of flowering involves iris – two groups of purple and two of white, three groups of herbaceous salvias in shades of blue, four groups of creamy yellow violas, two of dianthus, five shrub roses – pink ['Fantin Latour' and 'Mortimer Sackler'] and deep purple pink ['Tour de Malakoff' and 'Reine des Violettes']. There is a viticella clematis growing over 'Tour de Malakoff' because this rose doesn't repeat flower. Finally, the same colours are echoed with six groups of the *Dahlia* 'Le Baron' [see title page] and 'Cornish Ruby', together with later flowering Japanese anemones, cimicifugas, thalictrums, eupatoriums, echinops, saponiarias - and the annuals, *Nicotiana* 'Marshmallow' and *Cosmos* 'Candy Stripe'. There are six euphorbias [hybrids of characias] and they are quite a feature of this border … in spring they make a wonderful contrast with the pinks and purples, while the smoky foliage of the tree paeony, sedums and cimicifugas also provide a good foil." [See plant gallery on pages 126–27.]

The Acacia Border.
ABOVE: The border in April. *BELOW:* The border in June.

Spring

Tulipa 'Negrita'

Allium hollandicum 'Purple Sensation'

Astrantia 'Claret'

Lunaria annua (Honesty)

Summer

Rosa 'Fantin Latour'

Rosa 'Mortimer Sackler'

Rosa 'Reine des Violettes'

Late Summer

Anemone japonica

Cimicifuga 'Atropurpurea'

Dahlia 'Cornish Ruby'

Eupatorium purpureum

Spring

Euphorbia x *characias*

Chaerophyllum hirsutum 'Roseum'

Paeonia delavayi x *suffruticosa*

Thalictrum aquilegifolium

Summer

Rosa 'Tour de Malakoff'

Echinops ritro

Clematis viticella 'Odoriba'

Late Summer

Saponaria x *lempergei* 'Max Frei'

Thalictrum delavayi

Nicotiana mutabilis 'Marshmallow'

Cosmos 'Candy Stripe'

"So you have the same colour palette for the border, but it's achieved with different plants through the seasons?"

"Yes, that is what I aim for. So each bed or border in the garden features a different range of plants and colours. We do try to keep each bed looking good at all times, but hopefully each one should reach a 'best moment' at slightly different times during the year. It's also quite restful when some areas of the garden are looking quieter and maybe green becomes the dominant colour. Too much colour can be challenging – like too much food! If I have a favourite colour in the garden, it's green. In spring there are so many shades of green to enjoy and, perhaps, it is only as summer progresses and the greens are less vibrant - and the light is stronger – that the stronger colours come into their own. September is probably the most spectacular month in the garden. There is so much colour but by then it's softened by the sun being lower in the sky."

We then moved on to talk about the time some twenty years ago when Susie and Ian came to live at Coton. They came to take over the care of the garden after the unexpectedly early death of Haroldine, Ian's mother.

"I recall when we spoke some months ago you saying that the biggest challenge for you when you came here was learning the names of the plants, recognizing the plants – generally learning about plants."

"Well it was actually learning about what was in the garden because my gardening knowledge was limited to our London garden. My mother-in-law was a keen plantswoman and had access to a lot of very interesting plants through her friend, Valerie Finnis [RHS Victoria Medal of Honour, 1975]. It wasn't just taking on any old garden – it was a plantswoman's garden."

"And planted across several decades?"

"Yes, but Richard and Michael [Coton's gardeners at this time], who we inherited with the garden, so to speak, didn't really know much about plants either – they had only been used to planting them where Haroldine positioned them. They had never been consulted over them or indeed had to do the propagation of them because she had had a Head Gardener who did that."

"What was her name?"

"She was called Yvonne Daw, but she had left Coton two years previously to take up the job of Head Gardener at Cottesbrooke Hall. Her husband was the Head Gamekeeper there so it was a logical move. She had been here ten years. Richard and Michael had been my father-in-law's 'lieutenants', doing the mowing, hedging, looking after the birds and only occasionally popping a plant in the soil. My parents-in-law must have decided to manage without a Head Gardener. So we three had to try and sort out what these plants were. Ian's mother had left a plant list, but with no indication as to where the plants were in the garden. And there were quite a few notes about plants – mostly on the back of old envelopes – but in some cases it was pure guesswork, especially when it came to the variety names. I might have known it as a *Persicaria*, actually *Polygonum* in those days, but beyond that I had to look at the list, look at pictures and then try and work it out. In a sense at that stage I hadn't worked out what I have arrived at doing now … I was just beginning to understand what the plants were."

"It sounds like a steep learning curve."

"It takes a long time to learn the habits of plants. Well, they flower at different times of the year and for different lengths of time. Some need cutting back in order to repeat flower, which some will do quite quickly but others don't."

"How long did it take for you to acquire the knowedge, and the confidence, the wherewithal to change the planting? Was it a gradual process?"

"Very, very gradual."

"Are we talking decades?"

"We're talking the first ten years really. We've been here for 23 years now. I think that I wouldn't have been able to articulate my philosophy – my approach – until really the last eight or nine years."

"Really?"

"Yes, it's mostly been at a subconscious level because I wasn't learning it – well I was, but I was learning it for myself. It was just by observation and doing things."

"So how different do you think the garden is now to the one that you took over?"

"It's very difficult for me to be objective about it. It's not that different in terms of structure, but in terms of planting, it has changed enormously. But if I think about it we have changed quite a lot of the structure too – not a lot of the structure of the garden immediately round the house, although we put the box hedge in at the end of the pond. Richard did that so beautifully. Not so much close to the house but a lot elsewhere."

"Where have you changed the structure of the garden?"

"We've developed the more informal areas of the garden, extending the Woodland Garden, developing the Bog Garden, Herb Garden and Wildflower Meadow, and reinstalling a simpler rill. My husband's grandparents created the original structure of the garden around the house as you see it today and the fairly complex Water Garden. They also installed an ornamental rill running through the orchards on the way to the grass tennis courts at the bottom of the garden. They made a Kitchen Garden with greenhouses, a vinery and a potting shed, quite near the house, and they grew soft fruit – raspberries and gooseberries, I believe, in the lower part of the garden adjacent to the tennis courts. Ian's mother redesigned the Rose Garden, started the Woodland Garden and she planted the Rose Bank with old shrub roses below the formal part of the garden. My father-in-law removed the rill from the Old Orchard and made two ponds for his Emperor geese in the orchard enclosures. He and my mother-in-law merged half of a large arable field with the garden to form an area for his large collection of ornamental wildfowl. They named this area the Goose Park and they planted an interesting range of ornamental and fruit trees there.

"Is that where we see the flamingos and other birds wandering freely now?"

"Yes. After we had been here a couple of years, and following a prompt from Anthony du Gard Pasley - he was a landscape architect and a cousin of Ian's father - we started to dismantle the aviaries and enclosures containing birds, and the gates and field fences which had separated the Goose Park from the main part of the garden. We dispatched birds which had been housed in cages and those we didn't want to have free range of the garden, mainly geese, ornamental pheasants and peacocks. The removal of the field fences allowed us to establish the very large borders at the top of the Goose Park … and then we created a border at the bottom which we call the Meadow Border."

"Are there any other areas that you changed in your early years here?"

"The Herb Garden. That's where the henhouse used to be and it was rather scruffy. Richard designed this area and it's been very successful. He maintains it, and the Wildflower Meadow which he also created."

"What helped you most during that learning process, and was there anyone in particular that you tended to rely on?"

"Yes, there was this wonderful man called John Kimbell, who gardened with me for eight years. He was the one who said we needed to improve the soil. He was a real gardener with no professional training, but a lot of knowledge which he had acquired from his grandmother during his childhood. I think that hitherto copious amounts of leaf mould from the Bluebell Wood had been applied to the garden once a year, but I don't think much of it had been dug over. A lot of people don't believe in digging and rely on the worms to work the leaf mould down into the soil. But we garden on clay and if it's not improved, the soil can become compacted, sodden in winter and cracking in summer. John taught me the value of adding the burnt soil from underneath the bonfire, well-rotted muck and our own compost containing leaf mould as well as garden waste, and if necessary, some gravel. That's what we do now when we have an area of soil we need to improve. We do still mulch the borders with our own compost [contains leaf mould] when we have finished replanting them through the winter and spring, but we no longer use leaf mould from the Bluebell Wood as it introduces bluebells where we don't want them!"

"What about the poultry manure? Did Ian's parents use that from the chickens they bred for sale?"

"I really don't know. Ian has no recollection of it being used, which is odd because we put chicken pellets on various things in the garden now. It's one of the few things we add to the soil in terms of feeding it. We particularly use pellets around roses before they do their second flowering. Chicken pellets give a quick boost to plants."

"Looking back, the obvious question is what do you wish you'd done differently?"

"I'm not sure that there is anything specific that I would have wanted to do differently. There are a number of things which we have done and then changed over the years, and plants which haven't been put in the right place which have had to be moved and replanted or discarded altogether. It's now 23 years, which is a generation and a perfect time to reflect. It sounds like boasting, but some people who come here regularly say to me that we just keep making the garden better and better. Actually, I'm just refining my ideas all the time and I have had many years in which to keep attempting to 'improve' things. For example, the changes we completed in the Acacia Border this year have made such a difference … they have produced more space for me to play with. It hasn't meant going shopping for new things, but rather it's given everything sufficient space, which I think makes it all look so much better. People have been very generous in their comments about it."

"Who helps you most in the garden now?"

"Two people help me on a Monday, sometimes three on a Tuesday and three on a Thursday. Some of this help disappears during half terms and holidays! My principal helper, Sue [Mappledoram], is only here on Mondays and Tuesdays because she teaches for the rest of the week. I am on my own Wednesdays and Fridays, but I like it this way because it gives me time to think and plan. They are all interested and involved with the garden and have mostly been here for quite a long time. They are all looking forward to seeing the effect of the changes which we have made in the Acacia Border - they can't wait for next summer. This is why I find gardening such an inspiring occupation – anticipating seeing the results of work carried out maybe months before is such a stored-up pleasure."

Susie Pasley-Tyler and Sue Mappledoram: using Susie's notes for making changes to the Yellow and Blue Border, Autumn 2014.

"Was the Bluebell Wood open to the public during Haroldine's time?"
"I believe that when we took the garden over in 1991 the public had been visiting the Bluebell Wood for about 15 years. But it wasn't the sort of pilgrimage that it has since become for many people. We had to do quite a lot of work thinning out the beech trees, planting new ones where there were gaps … and we removed a number of larch trees. Because this introduced more light, the bluebells gradually improved and for many years now they have been a great draw. We believe that there have always been some bluebells in the wood, but the introduction of beech - probably planted by Ian's grandparents in the 1920s … it's not a native

tree in Northamptonshire – encouraged them to flourish. The beech leaves start to appear at the same time as the bluebell flowers – this creates a glorious harmony of lime green and blue, especially when the sun filters through the leaf canopy."

"You've removed some of the wild undergrowth in the Bluebell Wood. That would not have happened in Haroldine's time?"

"No, I don't think so. We have removed a considerable amount of bracken, bramble, holly and shrubby elder, which has cleaned the floor of the wood and now there is very little lower storey planting with the exception of a few holly bushes."

Lime-green and blue: Coton's Bluebell Wood in May.

"When did the Wildflower Meadow come about?"

"I reckon we sowed it about 20 years ago, but it took several years to become established … it's just that the years flash by and you forget. It was the sight of bare soil in high summer which prompted us to think it might be a good thing to do. You know we are a farm still, and in those days our farmer would always plough it up in August, so suddenly the sight of brown soil would hit you as you walked down the garden - it jarred. Wildflower meadows were just starting to feature in people's thinking in the early 1990s – perhaps not to the extent that they do now, but it was good to have something green beyond the garden and it also offered extra space for garden visitors to walk in."

"Is there anything new that you're planning for next year?"

"We're having a new table made for outside the dining room. It is a typical, slightly quirky Coton story. An elderly man who attended some of our garden school courses, but strangely never visited the garden at other times, was particularly interested in trees. He kindly gave us one or two really good specimens, a Wellingtonia and an Incense Cedar, amongst others.

When he died he left some money for us in his Will, along with gifts to many local charities. It was a very generous sum and since he had been such a tree enthusiast, we decided to have a table designed from a really good piece of seasoned oak. There had been a white, wrought iron table with a glass top outside the dining room. That had been the scene of many meals eaten outside during Ian's parents days at Coton. By the time we arrived here it didn't look very special and we dispatched it to the swimming pool area."

The 'Wainwright Table'.

"I remember you telling me that the windows there were enlarged so that you could walk through them to get to the recess outside."

"Yes, that was mainly to create more light inside the house, but as they were such large sash windows, we were able to bend to get underneath and go outside. These days we tend to walk round instead! For many years we just used this recess area for displaying pots of plants, but it occurred to us that it would be quite nice to have a table in this space again. We had seen a table at Great Dixter many years ago designed by Christopher and Nathaniel Lloyd which I discovered Richard had photographed. We are planning to design something along the same lines, with a bench on each side. It will be called the 'Wainwright Table' after John Wainwright because his generosity prompted this idea."

"So, what other things are you planning to change for next year?"

"I think one of the things that works in our favour is the size of this garden. It's not too big and I think that if we increased it any more, it would perhaps cross that threshold. One of the aspects that people seem to enjoy is the way the garden sits around the house – the fact that wherever they are, it's not too far back to the Café. It enjoys wonderful views out into the countryside on three sides and from almost every vantage point in the garden it's still possible to see the house, or some part of it. There are some gardens where you start to ask yourself 'have I already been down this bit?' because all the parts of the garden look similar to each other. Once you start to think like that it probably means the garden is becoming too repetitive – it can become boring."

"So it's not just size, it's balancing the different areas?"

"Yes, I think there is a tendency to think of gardens in terms of planting – borders and beds. But I think it is equally important to create breathing spaces in a garden, where people can rest their eyes and maybe themselves on a seat and contemplate. We are fortunate to have four quite large green areas within the garden – in the Woodland Garden, the lawns around the house, the Old Orchard and the Goose Park, and in addition, the Wildflower Meadow. There are also quite a few smaller and more intimate spaces around the garden as well as a number of very large borders. I hope that none of it is too repetitive or overwhelming."

"After more than 20 years' gardening here you're still very enthusiastic about it all."

"Oh, yes. Gardening for me seems on one level something like conducting an orchestra, less complicated than a real orchestra, but you have all the plants, like the instruments, performing differently with varying colours, shapes, heights, timings, and you have to attempt to keep them under control and bring them to perform as a whole. It is a constant challenge and totally absorbing! And I love it."

"So what is the joy for you?"

"It's just the pure pleasure of seeing things that work together - it lifts your spirit. It's like painting pictures all the time … yes, all the time, and quite often what works are things that you haven't engineered yourself, they just happen. I have been thinking about writing a book about the garden here for ages but never seem to have the time, and then you've come out of the woodwork, so to speak, which is wonderful. I was going to call this notional book 'Gardening to make you smile' because that's exactly what it does to me and I think everything about gardening is healthy and uplifting, isn't it? It's also very good to see other people smile when they see our garden …"

Susie at Coton, doing what she loves.

Afterword

Coton Manor Garden now welcomes many thousands of visitors a year. The majority make repeat visits but few know the history of the garden's creation. Now I've completed my research, I think the reason why we are all drawn to the garden is because in the 1920s Elizabeth and Harold Bryant had the foresight to let the site dictate its basic structure. No conflict ensued. Then their daughter, Haroldine, who understood plants, embellished this structure with skilful planting which sympathetically incorporated natural water sources thanks to the talents of her husband, Henry, the Commander. Another layer of loving care followed with Susie's superb eye for colour and texture, and her total commitment to allowing the garden to breathe and not overwhelm. Perhaps what enabled my mother and I to feel 'together' during our visits, despite her Alzheimers, was this continuity of loving care from three generations. We felt in harmony because the garden exudes it.

I have been struck by the number of people who have come to work at Coton Manor with the intention of only remaining for a short time, but then have changed their minds and stayed – or have repeatedly returned. It seems that it's not just the visitors who are drawn to Coton! Surrounded by the tranquillity and visual harmony of the garden, there can't be many better work locations, and how proud one must feel to be part of the team responsible for creating and maintaining its beauty.

So what of the future? When Coton Manor's current owner, Ian Pasley-Tyler, was asked this question, he replied: 'the next generation would be the fourth of my family at Coton. I have three children, a son and two daughters, who have shown varying degrees of interest in the garden. We are quietly confident that one of them will be sufficiently inspired by these surroundings to continue the work of previous generations'.

Meanwhile, the rhythm of life at the Manor continues. One year on from last year's first open day, I stand again at Coton's entrance gate whilst Ian and grandson, Harry, welcome the first visitors of 2015. Susie is as busy as ever in the garden. Harry has grown, the snowdrops have multiplied since last year to make an even more spectacular display, and visitors are eager to glimpse the first signs of spring. The vast majority of today's visitors have been to Coton before and it's as if they wish to revisit the garden as one would an 'old friend'. There's a strong sense of continuity, and somehow, it's all reassuringly familiar - and even though this book is now written and my home is far away in Monmouthshire, I too will return time and time again.

Dr Ann Benson. Monmouthshire, 2015.

Coton Plant List

Trees, shrubs and climbing plants are shown in capitals,
and for ease of reading, the use of italics is omitted.

Map of Coton Manor Garden

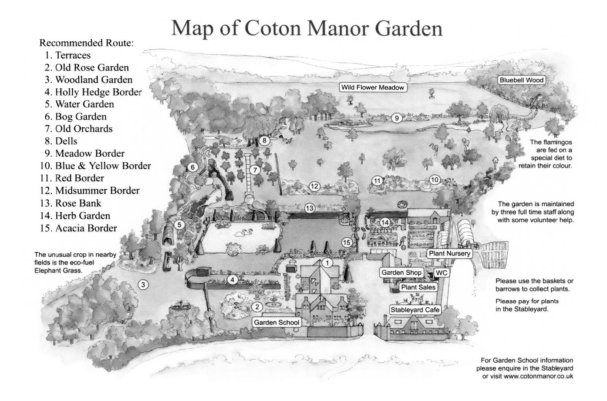

Recommended Route:
1. Terraces
2. Old Rose Garden
3. Woodland Garden
4. Holly Hedge Border
5. Water Garden
6. Bog Garden
7. Old Orchards
8. Dells
9. Meadow Border
10. Blue & Yellow Border
11. Red Border
12. Midsummer Border
13. Rose Bank
14. Herb Garden
15. Acacia Border

The unusual crop in nearby
fields is the eco-fuel
Elephant Grass.

Wild Flower Meadow

Bluebell Wood

The flamingos
are fed on a
special diet to
retain their colour.

The garden is maintained
by three full time staff along
with some volunteer help.

Plant Nursery

Garden Shop   WC

Plant Sales

Please use the baskets or
barrows to collect plants.

Please pay for plants
in the Stableyard.

Stableyard Cafe

Garden School

For Garden School information
please enquire in the Stableyard
or visit www.cotonmanor.co.uk

Acacia Border

Allium hollandicum 'Purple Sensation'
Althaea armenica
Anemone hupehensis 'Prinz Heinrich'
Anemone x hybrid 'Honorine Jobert'
Anemone x hybrid 'Robustissima'
Anemone x hybrid 'September Charm'
Astrantia 'Claret'
Astrantia 'Hadspen Blood'
Campanula burghaltii
Campanula lactiflora
Campanula 'Alba'
Campanula lactiflora
CARPENTERIA californica
Cimicifuga racemosa 'Atropurpureum'
CLEMATIS 'Alionushka'
CLEMATIS 'Huldine'
CLEMATIS 'Odoriba'
CLEMATIS 'Rebecca'
Clematis bonstedtii 'Crepuscule'
Clematis integrifolia
CLEMATIS montana 'Marjorie'
CLEMATIS 'Purpurea plena elegans'
Cynara cardunculus
Dahlia 'Cornish Ruby'
Dahlia 'Le Baron'
Dianthus 'Mrs Sinkins'
Echinops ritro
Eupatorium purpureum
Euphorbia characias wulfenii hybrids
Galega hartlandii 'Alba'
Geranium sanguineum striatum
Geranium sylvaticum 'Album'
Geranium sylvaticum 'Mayflower'
Hesperis matronalis
HYDRANGEA aspera sargentiana
HYDRANGEA macrophylla 'White Wave'
Iris 'Cliffs of Dover'
Iris mauve

Lavatera x clementii 'Bredon Springs'
Lobelia 'Russian Princess'
PAEONIA delavayi
PAEONIA delavayi f. lutea
PAEONIA mlokosewitschii
Penstemon 'Countess of Dalkeith'
Penstemon 'Raven'
Penstemon digitalis 'Husker's Red'
Penstemon pensham 'Plum Jerkum'
ROSA 'Bleu Magenta'
ROSA 'Mortimer Sackler'
ROSA 'Reine des Violettes'
ROSA 'Reve d'Or'
ROSA 'Tour de Malakoff'
ROSA centifolia 'Fantin Latour'
Salvia nemerosa 'Caradonna'
Salvia 'Peter Vigeon'
Salvia x pratensis 'Indigo'
Salvia x sylvestris 'May Night'
Saponaria x lempergeii 'Max Frei'
Sedum 'Vera Jameson'
Sedum matrona
Thalictrum aquilegifolium
Thalictrum delavayi
Thalictrum 'Elin'
Thalictrum rochebrunianum

Rose Garden

Agapanthus 'Blue Moon'
Agapanthus africanus 'Alba'
CARYOPTERIS x clanodensis
CERATOSTIGMA willmottianum
CLEMATIS texensis 'Princess Diana'
CLERODENDRUM trichotomum
Dahlia 'Geri Hoek'
Dianthus 'Gran's Favourite'

Dianthus 'Mrs. Sinkins'
Diascia fetcaniensis
Diascia integerrima
Eryngium bourgattii
Erysimum 'Constant Cheer'
Geranium renardii
Heuchera 'Chocolate Ruffles'
Iris pallida 'Argentea Variegata'

Knautia macedonica
Lavandula x intermedia 'Sawyers'
Libertia grandiflora
Lilium regale
Origanum laevigatum 'Herrenhausen'
Orlaya grandiflora
Paeonia 'Duchess de Nemours'
Paeonia 'Sarah Bernhardt'
Paeonia mloskewitschii
PAEONIA delavayii var. delavayi
PAEONIA emodi
Penstemon 'Apple Blossom'
Penstemon 'Hidcote Pink'
PHILLYREA angustifolia
ROSA 'Alfred de Dalmas'
ROSA 'Blush Noisette'
ROSA 'Cecile Brunner'
ROSA 'Francis Dubreuil'
ROSA 'Eden Rose'
ROSA 'Ellen Willmott'
ROSA 'Gardener's Pink'
ROSA 'Ghislaine de Feligonde'
ROSA 'Goldfinch'
ROSA 'Gruss an Aachen'
ROSA 'Little White Pet'
ROSA moschata 'Cornelia'

ROSA moschata 'Felicia'
ROSA 'Mrs Oakley Fisher'
ROSA multiflora 'Goldfinch'
ROSA 'Phyllis Bide'
ROSA 'St. Ethelburga'
ROSA banksia 'Lutea'
ROSMARINUS officinalis
Salvia 'Amistad'
Salvia greggii 'Pink Blush'
Salvia greggii 'Stormy Pink'
Salvia patens 'Guanajuato'
Salvia verticillata 'Purple Rain'
Sedum 'Bertram Anderson'
Sedum matrona

Blue and Yellow Border

Achillea 'Anthea'
Achillea 'Moonshine'
Aconitum carmichaelii 'Spatlese'
Aconitum carmichaelli 'Kelmscott'
Rhazya orientalis
Aster 'Purple Dome'
Aster x frikartii 'Wunder von Stafe'
Baptisia australis
Clematis heracleifolia 'Cassandra'
Dahlia 'Clair de Lune'
Dahlia pale yellow cactus
Digitalis ferruginea
Echinacea 'Sunrise'
Euphorbia wallichii
Galega 'His Majesty'
Geranium pratense 'Mrs Kendall Clarke'
Helenium 'Sahin's Early Flowerer'
Helianthus 'Lemon Queen'
Helianthus salicifolius
Hemerocallis 'Cream Drop'
Hemerocallis dumorteri
HYDRANGEA 'Limelight'
HYPERICUM inodorum 'Elstead'
Iris 'Dusky Skies'
Iris 'Rajah'

Kniphofia 'Green Jade'
Kniphofia 'Percy's Pride'
Lupinus 'Chandelier'
Lysimachia ciliata 'Firecracker'
Nepeta subsessilis
ROSA 'Maigold'
ROSA 'Graham Thomas'
Rudbeckia fulgida 'Goldsturm'
Salvia sylvestris 'May Night'
Salvia sylvestris 'Viola Klose'
Scabiosa ochraleuca
Thalictrum flavum glaucum
Thermopsis lanceolata
Verbena bonariensis

Holly Hedge Border

Aconitum carmichaelii 'Spatlese'
Aconitum napellus
Agapanthus campanulatus
Agapanthus 'Navy Blue'
Agapanthus 'Savile Blue'
Agastache foeniculum
Allium christophii
Anemone x hybrida 'Whirlwind'
Anemone x 'Honorine Jobert'
Anthericum liliago
Aster cordifolius 'Little Carlow'
Aster novae-angliae 'Autumn Snow'
Aster x frikartii 'Monch'
Astrantia major rosea
Baptisia australis
Campanula lactiflora
CEANOTHUS x delieanus 'Gloire de Versailles'
Chelone obliqua
Cimicifuga racemosa
CLEMATIS 'Marmori'
Clematis 'Petit Faucon'
Clematis recta
CLEMATIS viticella 'Betty Corning'
Clematis x durandii
Dahlia merckii
Delphinium 'Blue Bird'
Delphinium 'Summer Skies'
Delphinium elatum 'Finsteraarhorn'
FUCHSIA magellanica 'Mrs. Popple'
Galtonia candicans
LAVATERA 'Dorothy'
Lilium pardalinum
Lythrum salicaria 'Blush'
Penstemon 'King George'

Penstemon 'Snowstorm'
Persicaria amplexicaule 'Alba'
Phlox paniculata 'Blue Paradise'
Phlox paniculata 'Bright Eyes'
Phlox paniculata 'Europa'
Phlox paniculata 'Franz Schubert'
Phlox paniculata 'Luc's Lilac'
Phlox paniculata 'Mount Fuji'
ROSA 'Iceberg'
ROSA damascena 'Ispahan
ROSA Fred Loads'
ROSA 'Scarlet Queen Elizabeth'
Salvia microphylla var. microphylla
Salvia verticillata 'Purple Rain'
Stachys macrantha
Strobilanthes atropurpurea
Verbascum chaixi 'Album'
Veronica gentianoides
Veronica gentianoides 'Tissington White'
Veronicastrum virginicum

Water Garden

ACER palmatum 'Dissectum'
Allium 'Purple Sensation'
Anemone hupehensis 'Splendens'
Anemone x hybrida 'Honorine Jobert'
Anemone x hybrida 'Monterosa'
Astilbe 'Bressingham Beauty'
Astilbe 'Irrlicht'
Astilbe chinensis pumila
Astilbe simplicifolia 'Sprite'
Caltha palustris
CHOISYA ternata
Clematis integrifolia 'Pale Blue'
CLEMATIS viticella 'Polish Spirit'
Clematis x jouiniana
Dicentra spectabilis

Dierama 'Guinevere'
Euphorbia palustris
Euphorbia schillingii
Euphorbia wallichii
Hosta 'Thomas Hogg'
Hosta sieboldiana var. elegans
Iris 'Holden Clough'
Iris ensata 'Variegata'
Iris 'Gerald Darby'
Iris laevigata
Iris pseudacorus
Iris sibirica 'Ruffled Velvet'
Leucojum aestivum 'Gravetye Giant'
Ligularia przewalskii
Lobelia 'Hadspen Purple'

Lysichiton americanus
Lysimachia clethroides
Persicaria amplexicaule
Persicaria amplexicaule 'Album'
Persicaria bistorta 'Superbum'
Primula beesiana
Primula florindae
Primula japonica 'Miller's Crimson'
Primula Waltonii hybrids
Rodgersia pinnata 'Superbum'
Rodgersia quercifolia
ROSA 'Aimee Vibert'
ROSA gallica 'Versicolor'
ROSA Veilchenblau
Salvia Amistad
Saxifraga fortunei 'Wada's Variety'

VIBURNUM hillierii 'Winton'
WEIGELA 'Bristol Ruby'
WEIGELA 'Mont Blanc'
Zantedeschia 'Green Goddess'

Rose Bank

Achillea 'Cassis'
Achillea 'Summer Wine'
Achillea 'W B Child'
Achillea millefolium 'Cerise Queen'
Achillea millefolium 'Cherry King'
Allium sphaerocephalum
Artemisia canescens syn A. splendens
Artemisia ludoviciana
BUPLEURUM fruticosum
CEANOTHUS x delileanus 'Gloire de Versailles'
CLEMATIS 'Arabella'
CLEMATIS 'Romantika'
CLEMATIS 'Rouge Cardinal'
CLEMATIS viticella 'Polish Spirit'
Dianthus carthusianorum
Dianthus 'Laced Monarch'
Echinacea purpurea 'Kim's Knee High'
Echinacea purpurea 'Ruby Giant'
Echinacea purpurea 'Rubinstern'
Echinacea purpurea 'White Swan'
Eryngium bourgattii
Eryngium pandanifolium
Euphorbia characias wulfenii hybrids
Dianthus 'Memories'
Geranium cantabrigiense 'Biokovo'
Geranium clarkei 'Kashmir White'
Geranium libani
Geranium malviflorum
Geranium 'Mrs Kendall Clarke'
Geranium 'Patricia'
Geranium x oxonianum 'Walter's Gift'
Geranium x malviflorum 'Mavis Simpson'
Geranium x riversieaianum 'Russell Prichard'
Iris 'Elegans'
Iris 'Midnight Skies'
Iris 'Queechee'
Leucanthemum aglaia 'Alaska'
Leucanthemum aglaia 'Superba'
Melianthus major
PAEONIA delavayi x suffruticosa

PAEONIA rockii 'Highdown Strain'
PAEONIA rockii hybrid
Papaver orientale 'Cedric Morris'
Papaver orientale 'Royal Wedding'
Penstemon 'Abbotsmerry'
Penstemon 'Apple Blossom'
Penstemon 'Garnet'
Penstemon 'Raven'
ROSA 'Alan Titchmarsh'
ROSA 'Charles de Mills'
ROSA 'Ellen Willmott'
ROSA 'Empress Josephine'
ROSA 'Enfant de France'
ROSA 'Ferdinand Pichard'
ROSA 'Gertrude Jekyll'
ROSA 'Hermosa'
ROSA 'Honorine de Brabant'
ROSA 'Kazanlik'
ROSA 'Louise Odier'
ROSA 'Madame Pierre Oger'
ROSA 'Pearl Drift'
ROSA 'Quatre Saisons'
ROSA 'Redoute'
ROSA 'Rose de Rescht'
ROSA 'Sceptr'd Isle'
ROSA 'Sheelagh Baird'
ROSA 'Souvenir de La Malmaison'
ROSA 'Souvenir de Malmady'
ROSA 'St. Ethelburga'
ROSA alba 'Konigin von Danmark'
ROSA bonica
ROSA bourboniana 'Madame Isaac Pereire'
ROSA centifolia 'Fantin Latour'
ROSA chinensis 'Old Blush China'
ROSA gallica 'Versicolor'
ROSA moschata 'Penelope'
ROSA moschata 'Prosperity'
ROSA rugosa 'Alba'
ROSA rugosa 'Belle Poitevine'
ROSA rugosa 'Fimbriata'

ROSA rugosa 'Fru Dagmar Hastrup'
Salvia caradonna
Salvia certaposi
Salvia forsskaolii
Salvia var. neurepia 'Pink Blush'
Salvia interrupta
Salvia nemerosa ' Lubecca'
Salvia patens
Salvia sylvestris 'Blauhagel'
Salvia sylvestris 'May Night'
Sedum 'Frosty Morn'
Sedum 'Joyce Henderson'
Sedum 'Bertram Anderson'
Sedum erythrostictum 'Mediovariegatum'

Mediterranean Bank

Acanthus spinosus
Achillea millefolium 'Salmon Beauty'
Agapanthus 'Dokter Bronwer'
Agapanthus 'Headbourne Hybrids'
Agapanthus 'Midnight'
Agastache foeniculum
Agastache 'Red Fortune'
Agastache rupestris
Allium christophii
Asphodelus albus
Asphodelus lusitanicus
Astelia chathamica 'Silver Spear'
BUDDLEIA 'Dartmoor'
BUDDLEIA crispa
CISTUS 'Grayswood Pink'
CISTUS 'Alan Fradd'
Clematis 'Cassandra'
DAPHNE bholua 'Jacqueline Postill'
Diascia fetcaniensis
Eryngium agavifolium
Eryngium bourgatii
Eryngium pandanifolium
Erysimum 'Constant Cheer'
Euphorbia x martini
Euphorbia dulcis 'Chamaeleon'
Euphorbia myrsinites
Euphorbia x characias hybrid
Geranium 'Rozanne'
Geranium palmatum
Helianthemum 'Lawrenson's Pink'
Heuchera 'Amethyst'
Heuchera 'Palace Purple'
Heuchera 'Plum Pudding'
Iris 'Black' Jean P
Iris chrysophages Black Form
Iris 'Deep Black'
Iris 'Jane Phillips'
Iris mauve
LAVANDULA 'Hidcote Blue'
LAVANDULA 'Munstead Blue'

Libertia grandiflora
Morina longifolia
Nepeta 'Six Hills Giant'
OLEA europaea
Origanum 'Hopley's Variety'
Paeonia officinalis 'Alba'
Phlomis italicum
PHLOMIS 'Lloyd's Variety'
PIPTANTHUS laburnifolius
Potentilla hopwoodiana
POTENTILLA vilmorinii
ROSA glauca
ROSA 'Lady Emma Hamilton'
ROSA 'Meg'
ROSA 'Mrs Oakley Fisher'
ROSA 'Sweet Juliet'
Salvia greggii 'Blush Pink'
Salvia 'Purple Queen'
Salvia 'Senorita Leah'
SANTOLINA neapolitana 'Edward Bowles'
Schizostylis coccinea 'Jennifer'
Schizostylis coccinea 'Pink Princess'
Sedum 'Bertram Anderson'
Sedum 'Hab Grey'
Sedum 'Purple Emperor'
Sedum 'Red Cauli
Sedum ruprechtii

Meadow Border

Achillea millefolium 'Inca Gold'
Achillea millefolium 'Terracotta'
Achillea millefolium 'Walter Funcke'
Aconitum carmichaelii 'Kelmscott'
Aconitum carmichaelii 'Spatlese'
Agastache foeniculum
Agastache 'Blue Fortune'
Aster amellus 'King George'
Aster calliope
Aster cordifolius 'Little Carlow'
Aster x frikartii 'Jungfrau'
Aster x frikartii 'Wunder von Stafe'
BUDDLEIA lindleyana
Campanula lactiflora
Crocosmia 'Lady Hamilton'
Crocosmia 'Zambesi'
Dahlia orange cactus
Digitalis parviflora
Digitalis parviflora 'Milk Chocolate'
Echinacea purpurea 'Magnus'
Echinops ritro
Echinops ritro 'Veitch's Blue'
Eryngium planum
Eupatorium rugosum 'Chocolate'
Geranium 'Rozanne'
Geranium magnificum
Geum 'Dolly North'
Geum 'Princess Juliane'
Geum 'Totally Tangerine'
Helenium 'Sahin's Early Flowerer'
Helenium 'Septemberfuchs'

Helenium 'Zimbelstern'
HYPERICUM androsaemum 'Albury Purple'
Kniphofia 'Tawny King'
Kniphofia 'Tetbury Torch'
Kniphofia rooperi
Kniphofia caulescens
Ligularia dentata 'Desdemona'
Miscanthus sinensis 'Kleine Fontane'
Miscanthus sinensis 'Yakushima Dwarf'
Nepeta 'Longipes'
Nepeta 'Six Hills Giant'
Papaver orientale
Perovskia atriplicifolia
Potentilla 'William Rollison'
SAMBUCUS nigra 'Black Lace'
SORBUS 'JOSEPH ROCK'
Tulipa 'Ballerina'
Verbena bonariensis
Veronica petraea 'Pink Damask

Author's Acknowledgements

This book would not have been written without the help of many people. Coton Manor's current owners, Ian and Susie Pasley-Tyler, provided me with unlimited access to their collections of family photographs and memorabilia. Margaret Wilson gave information about E.F. Gill's painting of Coton Manor, which is now in her safe keeping. Men and women who have worked at the Manor, and those who continue to do so, have given generously of their time and memories. Some have dug deep into their experiences of more than half a century ago. I would particularly like to thank: Yvonne Daw, Richard Green, Charles Gregory, Sylvia Muddiman, Dennis Patrick, Sarah Patterson, Jean Reeder, Michael Simon, and Caroline Tait.

When I began to research Coton's history, Gren Hatton was incredibly generous in drawing my attention to hearth and sheep tax records. I am also indebted to the staff at Northampton Record Office and the British Library. Special thanks go to James Lowther, current owner of Holdenby House, for allowing me to read his own rare copy of Hartshorne's ancient history of Holdenby.

Mark Dragicevic of Addison Print, Northampton, was marvellously patient and diligent in laying out my work, and managed to bring all my ideas to fruition. Laura Brand at Berforts Information Press Ltd. at Stevenage came to my rescue when another printing company let me down. It was imperative that the book be available during May 2015, and Berforts' staff ensured this happened.

Lastly, thanks go to my friends for their forbearance and support throughout my quest for the history of Coton Manor.

Picture Credits

Unless otherwise stated, images are © Susie Pasley-Tyler and Michael Simon.

Preface

'The author's mother, Sophia Haywood (1916-2011)'. © Ann Benson.

Introduction

'Ian Pasley-Tyler and grandson, Harry, welcome the first visitors of 2014 to Coton'; 'The Wayman family: three generations of Coton visitors'; 'Sunshine and snowdrops'. © Ann Benson.

Domesday, Civil War and Restoration

'Medieval settlements and estates: Cottesbrooke, Creaton, Guilsborough, Hollowell and Ravensthorpe'. Taken from *History and Antiquities of the County of Northampton*, George Baker (London: Bower Nicols & Son and Rodwell, 1822-1830), p.xiv.

'The Dickens' Crest'. © Dennis Patrick.

'The impact of the New Model Army on Northamptonshire parishes in June 1645'. Taken from *Naseby, the Decisive Campaign*, Glenn Foard (Barnsley: Pen and Sword Military, 2004), p.170.

'The part of Holdenby House left standing by Baynes' and 'Drawing of the screen showing the metope frieze with its rosettes'. Taken respectively from *Historical Memorials of Northampton*, Albert and Charles Hartshorne (London: Harrison and Sons, 1908), p.12 and p.60.

'Stone over-mantle at Coton'; 'Commemorative bucranium decorations on Holdenby's 1904 building'; 'Rosette on downpipes at Holdenby House'; 'Screen in Holdenby's Church'; 'Rosette on the 1662 gable end of Coton Manor'; 'Iron-stone and oölite: Holdenby's estate cottages; Coton Manor'; 'Coton's old farmhouse kitchen, now a sitting room, in the 1662 part of the manor house'. © Ann Benson.

'Manor of Coton Suit Roll 27th October 1721'; Northamptonshire Record Office (NPL 1439).

'Court Roll of 1692 listing Michael Hollis of Coton'; Northamptonshire Record Office (CAM 1036). 'Map of the County of Northampton (London: Greenwood, Pringle & Co., 1826)';

Northamptonshire Record Office. 'Map of Coton by William Bonsor, 1839'; Northamptonshire Record Office. 'Section of the First Edition Ordnance Survey map of Coton, 1885'; London, British Library.

'Painting of Coton Farm, 1894'. Taken from the painting, *Coton Grange Farm*, F.G.Gill, 1894. © Margaret Wilson.

Elizabeth and Harold Bryant

Cricket XI, 1893, Repton School, Derbyshire. © Repton School, Derbyshire.

'Lake Worth, Palm Beach County, Florida'. Taken from *The Wonder Atlas of the World,* (London: The Literary Press Ltd.) p.21.

'Haroldine's riding accident'; '10 August 1934'; '20 May 1938'; '14 May 1938'. © *Mercury and Herald.*

Haroldine and the Commander

'The selling of ducks in full swing'; 'Coton: poultry farm and market garden'. © *Mercury and Herald.*

'The same area, 2014: 'rearing' of a different kind'. © Caroline Tait.

'Dennis and the bench that was moved from the stone wall where he installed the fountain fifty years ago'; 'Dennis by the well-head under the chestnut tree'; 'Coton's Florentine well-head in the Rose Garden'; 'Alfie and little Marmaduke'; 'Haroldine and Henry, the Commander: a tribute'. © Ann Benson.

'Cantoria by Lucca della Robbia, 1431-38; Museo dell'Opera del Duomo, Florence'. © Penny Howard.

Susie and Ian Pasley-Tyler

'Charles teaches Susie how to graft'; 'Apple trees being grown on in France, 1993. © Charles Gregory.

'Setting out the trees in the Car Park Orchard, 1994'. © Jean Reeder.

'Fruition'; 'Wildflower Meadow: plug plants being inserted and film crew in action'; 'Caroline Tait producing plants at Coton Manor'; 'The floor being laid in the new potting shed'; 'Gardening at Coton during the winter months: Susie Pasley-Tyler and Sue Hill refresh the borders in the late-1990s'; 'Caroline Tait's propagation class'; 'Michael and Richard gutting the greenhouse, 2007'; 'Longhorn cows at Coton, 2014'. © Caroline Tait.

'Rodney at home in the Kitchen Garden, 2015'; 'Richard Green, Head Gardener at Coton Manor'; 'Herb Garden and Rose Walk, 2014'; 'The Plant Nursery with greenhouses, 2015'; 'Secluded seating area'; 'One of Richard Green's plant supports in Coton's garden'; 'Tom Duncan's talk on Irish Gardens, 2014'; 'Sarah Patterson welcoming people to a Garden School event, coffee on hand'; 'Pan, by Mary Cox'; 'Temperate House now used to sell tender plants'; 'Wall fountain repositioned outside the greenhouse'; 'Yews showing re-growth after Richard's hard pruning in 2013'; 'Refurbished plant storage / selling area, 2015'; 'Sylvia making jam'. © Ann Benson.

Every effort has been made to trace copyright holders and apologies are offered in advance for any unintentional omissions or errors, which would be corrected without hesitation in any subsequent edition of the book.